AF718847

KF
4137
Z9S65
1929a

WITHDRAWN

A10201 321989

Columbia University

Contributions to Education

Teachers College Series

No. 349

AMS PRESS
NEW YORK

LEGAL LIMITATIONS ON THE RIGHTS AND POWERS OF SCHOOL BOARDS WITH RESPECT TO TAXATION

By

WAYNE W. SOPER, Ph.D.

Teachers College, Columbia University
Contributions to Education, No. 349

Bureau of Publications
Teachers College, Columbia University
NEW YORK CITY
1929

Library of Congress Cataloging in Publication Data

Soper, Wayne Wellington, 1891-
Legal limitations on the rights and powers of school boards with respect to taxation.

Reprint of the 1929 ed., issued in series: Teachers College, Columbia University. Contributions to education, no. 349.
Published also as thesis, Columbia.
Bibliography: p.
1. School districts--United States--Finance.
2. Property tax--United States. I. Title.
II. Series: Columbia University. Teachers College. Contributions to education, no. 349.
KF4137.Z9S65 1972 344'.73'076 79-177759
ISBN 0-404-55349-4

Reprinted by Special Arrangement with Teachers College Press, New York, New York

From the edition of 1929, New York
First AMS edition published in 1972
Manufactured in the United States

AMS PRESS, INC.
NEW YORK, N. Y. 10003

ACKNOWLEDGMENTS

The writer wishes to express his appreciation to those who have helped make this study possible. To many members of the administration of education group of which he was a member he owes a debt of gratitude for individual and group criticisms. To his dissertation committee, Prof. N. L. Engelhardt, Prof. Carter Alexander, and Dr. John S. Brubacher, he wishes to express his gratitude for assistance during the progress of the study and for criticism of the completed manuscript. Particularly is he indebted to Dr. N. L. Engelhardt, chairman of the committee, for suggestions, criticisms and, above all, for encouragement during the whole course of the study. Dr. George D. Strayer assisted with valuable suggestions and criticisms, for which the author is grateful. Finally, to his wife, Venice Hitchcock Soper, who accepted a heavier home responsibility and offered continual encouragement, does he wish to express his extreme gratitude.

W. W. S.

CONTENTS

LEGAL LIMITATIONS ON THE RIGHTS AND POWERS OF SCHOOL BOARDS WITH RESPECT TO TAXATION

CHAPTER I

INTRODUCTION

Public institutions and taxation are coeval. Provision for the former depends upon the possibility of the latter. Public institutions depend upon general taxation for their perpetuity. Philanthropies have never in the history of nations been able to support institutions whose purpose is to promote the general welfare of a large majority of the people, because wealth never has been voluntarily offered in large enough contributions to meet the public needs of society. Where large amounts of the national wealth have been available through the power of taxation, public institutions have flourished; under conditions wherein wealth has not been procurable in the form of taxation, those institutions have faltered.

The rise of modern nations has witnessed an increase both in the number and in the extent of public institutions, together with an attendant increase in public taxation. Public education in this country annually demands no small portion of the public revenue for its support. With increasing demands for funds with which to provide additional facilities in the nation's schools has come the necessity for numerous legislative enactments to furnish the necessary legal machinery whereby more funds would become available. Of necessity, many such laws are general in their nature. Furthermore, the creation of and the provision for the support of a public institution by statutory enactment are but the first steps in the proper functioning of the institution. Laws are never so perfect as to prevent misunderstanding of their complete intent and operation; individuals and groups are never in such complete agreement as to obviate different interpretations of the law. It is here that the courts render their greatest service. A statement from one of their own justices emphasizes the argument: [1]

> They [laws] are perhaps deficient in precision and clearness, but however faulty or imperfect in phraseology or structure, we are bound to give them such an interpretation as may appear best adapted to effectuate the object contemplated. . . . When the design of the Legislature is not clearly apparent, it is always to be presumed they intended that the most reasonable and beneficial interpretation should be given to the language which they have used.

Judicial interpretations have built up a body of precedents which enables individuals and groups to predict the legal consequences of their acts. While the legal highway may have occasional detours due to a change of legislation or a reversal of policy, its precedents are well-marked signboards which the layman can use to reach a certain destination in his interpretation of performed or contemplated acts.

The Problem

Since the only proper way of raising money for public school purposes is by taxation,[2] it is obligatory that those responsible for the management and conduct of the public schools know the powers they possess and the limitations upon those powers. Court decisions constitute an important phase of the law of public school administration. Heretofore much emphasis has been placed upon legislative enactments to the neglect of the final decisions pertaining to those enactments. The law itself may be general, or it may be ambiguous, or it may need to be construed in the light of particular circumstances. Under such conditions it may be meaningless until properly construed by a court of law. The courts attempt to discover and formulate general principles out of the maze of legislative enactment; and in this way, judicial decisions have come to reveal in a highly significant manner the relation of the state to education.[3] These decisions extend into every legal phase of the educational program.

This problem resolves itself into the following contemplated discoveries:

[1] Pickering *v.* Day, 3 Houston (Del.) 474, Chief Justice Galpin.

[2] Sugar *v.* Monroe, 108 La. 677; Herald *v.* Board of Education, 65 W. Va. 765.

[3] Edwards, I. N. *Elementary School Journal,* 23 : 435.

1. To discover standards and rules which are recognized and applied by judicial tribunals, from cases which have come before the courts, regarding the raising of funds for public school purposes,
2. To point out the conditions under which such standards and rules will be applied in litigation, and
3. To reveal to boards of education their powers and liabilities with respect to taxation for the support of education.

In spite of constitutional provisions and legislative enactments defining the powers of boards of education, much litigation has arisen over the rights and powers of such boards in matters of taxation. To determine the trend of court decisions with the possibility of preventing much expensive litigation is one purpose of the study. It is not to be expected, however, that a brief study, such as this must necessarily be, can take cognizance of more than the general principles laid down by the courts. Where unusual circumstances and conditions render a different interpretation to a statute, it will not be possible to analyze all the implications of such a case. The study does not purport to be a means for getting out of entanglements over matters of taxation, but contemplates a means of avoiding many of the difficulties in which boards of education are so often involved.

Boards of education are composed of lay members, who, from the very nature of their diverse occupations, are not familiar with nor cognizant of many of their rights and powers as boards of public education. In so far as possible, this study attempts to formulate in as simple a manner as possible those rights and powers as such pertain to taxation. Furthermore, the reader is advised not to anticipate comment and proffered opinion on what the statutes and the court decisions should say and do, but merely to expect the revelation of principles and rules as formulated and applied. The question never is, How should the courts construe the law? but, How do they? Regardless of how boards of education and school administrators might wish to project their opinions into court decisions, they have no power to do so. The most that can be done is to acquire a fundamental knowledge of existing constitutional and statutory law and the general principles which the courts will follow in construing those laws. This knowledge should be exceedingly useful in a smoother administration of the public schools.

In order to make the discoveries before mentioned and to acquaint school boards and administrators with their powers and liabilities in matters of taxation, the case law method of attack has been selected as the one best adapted to the purposes of the study. Obviously, it is impossible to confine a complete study of the law of taxation as contained in the statute books of every state to one small volume. A mere tabulation of the provisions of the laws of each state referring to taxation for the support of public schools would be a prodigious task. Yet out of the mass of laws the courts have enunciated many definite principles, the large majority of which are supported by a preponderant weight of authority, with only here and there divided opinion. Case law has reference to the decided cases that have come before the various law tribunals for adjudication. Since no case is definitely settled until it has reached the highest tribunal in its jurisdiction, cases reaching the supreme courts of the various states have been resorted to. In addition to these, cases reaching the federal courts have been used wherever discovered, together with a few other unreversed decisions of inferior courts. Another reason for using cases of the state supreme courts is that the decisions of a court of inferior jurisdiction are not binding upon a superior court. It sometimes happens that courts reverse the decisions of a lower court and in some instances have overruled their own decisions when it has been discovered that great injustice has been rendered or changed conditions have outgrown the interpretation previously made.

While the decisions of the court of last resort in one state are not binding on a different state, it very often happens that courts of one state follow the rulings of other states. Particularly is this true when cases at bar involve similar points at issue. The Supreme Court of the United States commonly follows the decisions of the state supreme courts unless it is shown that their interpretations are repugnant to the Federal Constitution or some federal statute.

The number of cases on taxation that have passed through

the courts of the United States since the establishment of the federal union are legion. They embrace every phase and ramification of taxation. Those in which a school district has been a party are exceedingly numerous. The latter have been employed for the most part in this study, but have been supplemented by other cases on taxation when a general principle applicable alike to any political subdivision was deducible. The parties to the case are not so important as the issues involved.

The study has two widely different applications. First, the erection of danger signals beyond which boards of education and school administrators should not venture; second, the construction of improved highways reaching to points not at present utilized by school authorities, but entirely within their rights and powers. The first may be said to define the powers that boards now have or think they have and to confine them to such powers. The second attempts to emphasize heretofore unused powers and to encourage the use of those powers. An illustration will clarify the statement—an attempt to levy taxes on property not within the school district renders such levy void. A knowledge of this principle serves to deter a board of education from attempting to make such a levy. This illustrates the first application. Property exempt from taxation under constitutional or statutory provision may be sold to one in whom the exemption privilege is not vested, and becomes then subject to taxation. School authorities should assert their right to levy taxes on such property as assessable for the support of education rather than to assume that once exempt it is always exempt. This illustrates the second application.

Limitations of the Problem

Since a previous study [4] admirably organized the principles relative to rights and liabilities with respect to capital outlay contracts, this study does not embody the phase of taxation directly concerned with capital outlay expenditures. Rather has it been more confined to taxation cases wherein general taxation for current expenditures has been involved. Where

[4] Henzlik, F. E. *Rights and Liabilities of Public School Boards Under Capital Outlay Contracts.* Bureau of Publications, Teachers College, Columbia University, 1924.

the same principles have been deducible, however, both types of cases have been cited.

Cases wherein difficulties arising over the expenditure of school funds constitute the issue are very numerous as are those involving the use of school property for other than school purposes. In fact, the use of school property for other than school purposes is commonly challenged on the ground that such use is a purpose not contemplated by the tax statute. In so far as the cases used in this study directly involve the expenditure of revenue raised by taxation that phase of the problem has been incorporated, but only in a brief chapter. The use of school property for other than school purposes has not been included. Those desiring a brief but comprehensive discussion of this phase are referred to Trussler's [5] *Essentials of School Law.*

The study is not a treatise on taxation. It attempts to deal with only the legal principles as derived from court decisions. The opening up of new orifices of the public purse, the incidence of taxation, and like topics are not a part of the present study. Likewise, no attempt has been made to discuss the different kinds of taxes, such as, poll, income, inheritance, corporation, and decedent's property taxes. The term, tax, as employed, is that defined by courts of law. It is an enforced contribution of money or property, assessed in accordance with some reasonable rule of apportionment by authority of a sovereign state on persons or property within its jurisdiction for the purpose of defraying the expenses of government.[6]

Many more cases have been examined than are cited in the footnotes of this study. Those persons interested in other cases than the ones included here are referred to the law digests.

[5] Trussler, Harry R. *Essentials of School Law.* Bruce Publishing Co., Milwaukee, Wis.

[6] New Jersey *v.* Anderson, 203 U. S. 483; Redmond *v.* Tarboro, 106 N. C 122; Pollock *v.* Farmers' Loan, etc., Co., 157 U. S. 429; Foster *v.* Stevens, 63 Vt. 175; Aetna Fire Ins. Co. *v.* Jones, 78 S. C. 445.

CHAPTER II

THE NATURE AND THE SOURCE OF THE TAXING POWER OF THE SCHOOL DISTRICT

Derivation of the Power to Tax

That education is a public duty is now indisputable. Not only is this fact supported by the best educational thought, but it is also written into constitutions and upon statute books, and is upheld by a long, unbroken line of court decisions. A second and equally axiomatic proposition is that education is a function of the state.[1] The Tenth Amendment to the Federal Constitution implies this proposition. State constitutions invariably embody a clause or clauses providing for the education of the state's future citizenry; and legislatures have enacted numerous laws to carry out the intent of the constitutions. In order to perform the function of educating its future citizens more efficiently, the states early delegated much of the authority and control of education to political subdivisions—sometimes to the county, frequently to the township, and quite commonly to the school district. This delegation was not a surrender of the control of education but an operation of that power through agencies responsible to the state. The question, therefore, arises, In this delegation of authority to the local subdivisions was the power of taxation included? A brief review of the source of the taxing power will furnish the answer. In this review, the school district—not other political subdivisions—is emphasized.

The school district or other local subdivision authorized to

[1] The courts have consistently held to the opinion that education is a state and not a local function. Excerpts from a few decisions will show the general trend of opinion. The supreme court of Connecticut (Walsh *v.* Hine, 59 Conn. 50) says, "The duty of providing for the education of the children was regarded as a duty resting upon the state." Indiana (State *v.* Howarth, 122 Ind. 462) decided that "every school that has been established owes its existence to legislation; and every school officer owes his authority to the state." The supreme court of Arkansas held (State *v.* Atchison, T. & S. F. Ry., 28 Ark. 84) that "The mandate of the constitution to establish and maintain public schools throughout the state is directed to the legislature of the entire state, and not to any political subdivisions."

conduct the schools has no inherent power of taxation.[2] The power of taxation is inherent in a sovereign state.[3] That power is not generally conceived of as even being granted by the constitution of the state but of necessity underlies it because government could not exist without it. The constitution, however, may surround the power with limitations; otherwise, the power would be unlimited so far as the sovereign state itself is concerned. By unanimous decision over a long period of years, this inherent power of taxation falls to the legislative department of government.[4] In Preston *v.* Sturgis Milling Co., District Judge Cochran, quoting Justice Field in a previous similar case, says: [5]

'In the distribution of powers of government in this country into three departments the power of taxation falls to the legislature. It belongs to that department to determine what measures shall be taken for the public welfare and to provide the resources for the support and administration of the government throughout the state and all its subdivisions. Having sole power to authorize the tax, it must equally possess the sole power to prescribe the means whereby the tax shall be collected and to designate the officers through whom it shall be enforced.'

That the power and authority to levy taxes is an unusual one and deserving of careful safeguarding is indicated in the following language, spoken by Justice Cunningham in a Kansas case: [6]

The authority to levy taxes is an extraordinary one. It is never left to implications unless it be a necessary implication. Its warrant must be found in the act of the legislature. Any other rule might lead to great wrong and oppression and when there is a reasonable doubt as to its existence the right must be denied.

[2] Lane *v.* City of Unadilla, 114 S. E. (Ga.) 636; Chicago, B. & Q. R. Co. *v.* School Dist. No. 57 of Kearney County, 194 N. W. (Nebr.) 479; Berrier *v.* Board of Commissioners of Davidson County, 120 S. E. (N. C.) 328.

[3] McCulloch *v.* Maryland, 4 Wheat 428; Nathan *v.* Louisiana, 12 U. S. (L. ed.) 997; Lane County *v.* Oregon, 19 U. S. (L. ed.) 104; Humphrey *v.* Peques, 21 U. S. (L. ed.) 328; Board of Liquidation *v.* McComb, 92 U. S. 535; Hodge *v.* Richmond, 99 U. S. 355; United States *v.* Snyder, 149 U. S. 214; People *v.* Coleman, 4 Cal. 46; People *v.* McCreery, 34 Cal. 432; State *v.* Smith, 158 Ind. 543; People *v.* Reardon, 184 N. Y. 431, affirmed 204 U. S. 152.

[4] Talbot *v.* Janson, 1 U. S. (L. ed.) 553; Ware *v.* Hylton, 1 U. S. (L. ed.) 582; Meriweather *v.* Garrett, 102 U. S. 515; Spencer *v.* Merchant, 125 U. S. 355; State *v.* Smith, *supra*, note 3; State Tax Commissioners *v.* Holiday, 150 Ind. 216; Commonwealth *v.* Kennedy, 118 Ky. 618; People *v.* Brooklyn, 4 N. Y. 419; State *v.* Thorpe, 112 Wis. 81.

[5] 183 Federal 1.

[6] M. and McP. R. Co. *v.* Alexander, 63 Kan. 72.

Thus we are brought squarely to the fact that taxation is a state function. The legislature is the branch of government which exercises that function. No political subdivision can exercise this power only as such may be delegated to it. The taxing power of a state is one of its attributes of sovereignty and where there has been no compact with the federal government nor cession of jurisdiction for the purposes specified in the constitution, this power reaches all property and business within the state.[7]

Constitutional Requirements

In many of the state constitutions, if not in all, there are provisions for a general and uniform system of common schools. The legislature is directed to provide for the establishment, support, and management of such educational facilities. When constitutions so provide, they do not mean that the state must directly and by statute levy taxes for each locality, nor that it shall prescribe rules and regulations for every school district in the state. What is generally meant is that the legislature shall by general law provide for conducting schools and securing revenue with which to support them.[8] It is quite obvious that the legislature must employ agencies to conduct the schools. These agencies are purely creatures of the state and derive their powers from the state.[9] Constitutional restrictions are for the most part confined to the requirements that taxes shall be uniform and equal, which is construed to mean that no class of subjects or property shall be discriminated against or favored in the levying and collecting of taxes. Even with such provisions, there remains for the legislature to prescribe what means of taxation are equal and uniform, which in turn must be fully interpreted by courts of law. It therefore follows that unless a state constitution expressly restricts or forbids certain kinds or methods of taxation the legislature is equipped with plenary power to act within its own discretion.

[7] Duer *v.* Small, Fed. Cas. No. 4, 116.

[8] Robinson *v.* Schenck, 102 Ind. 307.

[9] Pearson *v.* State, 56 Ark. 148; State *v.* Hine, 59 Conn. 50; Chambers *v.* State, 127 Ind. 365; State *v.* Freeman, 61 Kan. 90; Minsinger *v.* Rau, 236 Pa. St. 327; Malone *v.* Williams, 118 Tenn. 390; Honaker *v.* Board of Education, 42 W. Va. 170.

Extent of the Taxing Power

Just to what extent may the legislature go in providing for public revenue for schools by means of taxation? In Anderson *v.* Ritterbusch,[10] the court, among other things, said:

> The taxing power, acting within its legitimate sphere, is one that knows no stopping place until it has accomplished the purpose for which it exists, namely, the actual enforcement and collection from every object of taxation of its proportionate share of the public burdens; and if prevented for any reason it may return again and again until . . . the tax is collected.

As this taxing power is legislative, however, it can be exercised only under legislative authority and each step in the process from beginning to end must be taken only as the legislature may prescribe.[11] It has been held in most jurisdictions that the amount of taxes and the rate of taxation are exclusively for the legislative body to prescribe, and may be increased or decreased at its pleasure, subject only to such restrictions as are imposed by state and federal constitutions. And the amount and rate may be increased by any method the lawmaking body may adopt, subject only to constitutional requirements.[12]

Nor is the legislature's power over schools exhausted by exercise, and the fact that a legislature has always intrusted the management of the schools of the state to local authorities will not preclude it at any time from changing the system so as to remove the schools from local control. The legislature may from time to time, in its discretion, abolish school districts, or enlarge or decrease them, or increase, modify, or abrogate their powers.[13] While the principle upon which taxation is to be imposed by the state is very often pointed out by the constitution, the extent to which it may be carried is left unlimited, except by legislative discretion.[14] It has even been ruled that

[10] 98 P. (Okla.) 1002.

[11] Preston *v.* Sturgis Milling Co., 183 F. 1.

[12] People *v.* Board of Review of Cook County, 125 N. E. (Ill.) 274; *in re* McKennan's Estate, 25 S. D. 369.

[13] Pass School Dist. *v.* Hollywood School Dist., 156 Cal. 416; Winona *v.* School Dist. No. 82, 40 Minn. 13; Edmondson *v.* Board of Education, 108 Tenn. 557.

[14] Stockton, etc., R. Co. *v.* Stockton, 41 Cal. 149; People *v.* Hussey, 4 Cal. 46; Gautier *v.* Ditmar, 129 N. Y. S. 834.

as the power of taxation is an attribute of sovereignty it may be exercised to such an extent as to embarrass and even destroy unless restrained by the organic law.[15]

Can the legislature, either acting for itself or through its agencies, impose a tax upon a locality without the consent of the people of that locality or in opposition to their wish? The answer to this question will be found in two typical cases. In Eicholtz *v.* Martin,[16] certain taxpayers brought an action to prevent the collection of taxes levied for the erection of a high school and its maintenance, claiming that the taxes levied were unconstitutional and void since no legal notice was ever given of an election to establish the high school and no election was ever held for that purpose by the trustees of such high school. The question before the court was, Was it competent for the legislature to determine whether a general law could be made applicable, and whether a special law was necessary? The court upheld the validity of the special act creating the high school district, in spite of the taxpayers' opposition. A few pertinent words of the presiding judge are:

> If the question were a new one, the writer of this opinion would be inclined to the view that the courts should determine in each case whether this constitutional restriction had been violated or not; but the question has been put at rest by a long series of decisions holding that the decision of the question is exclusively for the legislature and not for the courts.

The second case[17] is similar. It was an original proceeding in mandamus to compel county commissioners to carry out provisions of an act respecting the establishment of a high school. The contention of the commissioners was that the county cannot be compelled to build a high school and maintain it without the consent of those who are to pay for it and that the legislature exceeded its power when it attempted to impose such a task and burden upon them. The court said in part with reference to the issue:

> The matter of education is one of public interest which concerns all the people of the state and is therefore subject to the control of the

[15] Van Deman & Lewis Co. *v.* Rast, 214 F. 827.

[16] 53 Kan. 486; further citations on the same issue—Elevator Co. *v.* Stewart, 50 Kan. 378; State *ex rel v.* Hitchcock, 1 Kan. 178.

[17] State *v.* Freeman, 61 Kan. 90.

legislature. While education is a matter of state concern, the high school being especially beneficial to the people of the community in which it is established, the burden of maintaining it may be rightfully cast upon them. It is conceded that the legislature has full power to compel local organizations of the state to maintain common schools, and as schools of higher grade are authorized by the constitution no reason exists why such organizations may not be compelled to maintain such schools.[18]

As to subjects and property taxable, the legislature has power to tax all property and subjects within its jurisdiction unless expressly prevented by organic law.[19] Abundant authority therefore exists investing the legislature with plenary power in all matters of taxation, the only restrictions necessary of observance being those found in the constitutions of either the state or the federal government.[20]

Delegation of the Power to Tax

Since the power of taxation is an attribute of a sovereign state and not of its political subdivisions and is exercisable by the state legislature, by virtue of what right may school districts through their officers provide funds for the support of schools? It has already been stated that the constitutions of the states do not require that the legislature prescribe for each district separately. In like manner, it has been intimated that the state performs its function of educating its children through agencies to whom it delegates the necessary powers.

Is the sovereign power of taxation delegable? If so, is it delegable to school districts? The burden is upon every political subdivision which demands taxes from the people to show the authority to exercise such power in the manner in which it has been imposed.[21] It is apparent, therefore, that school districts must be responsible through their boards of education for the power of taxation they exercise. Any one questioning such authority possesses the right to demand proof of its existence.

As a general rule, sovereign power cannot be delegated by the

[18] *See also* Koester *v.* Commissioners of Atchison County, 44 Kan. 141; State *v.* Commissioners of Shawnee County, 28 Kan. 431.

[19] State *v.* Fidelity and Deposit Co. of Maryland, 80 S. W. (Tex.) 544; Robertson *v.* State Land Office Commissioner, 6 N. W. 659; Parker *v.* Winsor, 5 Kan. 362; Johnson *v.* Bradley-Watkins Co., 120 Ky. 136.

[20] For a complete discussion of the territorial limitations of the taxing power of the legislature, see Chapter III.

[21] Lane *v.* City of Unadilla, 114 S. E. (Ga.) 636.

legislature. An exception exists, however, in the case of minor political subdivisions, since the state must exercise many of its powers and functions through such agencies. Since school districts are created to assist the state in carrying out its function of education, they are commonly vested with the power of taxation.[22] Such power is usually conferred upon the district expressly or by necessary implication by constitutional, charter, or statutory provisions,[23] the nature and extent of such power depending upon the terms of the particular provisions relating thereto.[24] Under a few jurisdictions the legislature has no power to delegate taxation to school district authorities,[25] while in others the legislature cannot impose a tax except through the agency of local authorities.[26] But in most jurisdictions, subject to constitutional limitations and restrictions, the legislature may delegate the power of taxation to school districts.[27] The power thus granted may be exercised only as expressly or impliedly authorized by the provisions granting such power,[28] since the right of a school district to levy a tax, if it exists at all, must clearly be found in the statute. If there is a fair doubt as to its existence, it must be denied.[29] School district boards have no powers of taxation except those conferred upon them and any doubtful claims are resolved against them.[30] Nor can they bind the district for acts which are not within the scope of their authority.[31] Taxes levied without authority are void.

[22] McLoud *v.* Selby, 10 Conn. 39; Freel *v.* Crawfordsville School City, 142 Ind. 27; Kuhn *v.* Board of Education, 175 Mich. 438; Pittsburg *v.* Sterrett Subdist. School, 204 Pa. St. 635; Howard *v.* Tacoma School Dist., 88 Wash. 167.

[23] Marion, etc., R. Co. *v.* Alexander, 63 Kan. 72; Ogden Board of Education *v.* Brown, 12 Utah 251; Hogg *v.* Rogers, 15 U. C. C. P. 417.

[24] Davis *v.* Ponder, 131 Ga. 713; Lane *v.* Stanly, 65 N. C. 153; Bull *v.* Read, 13 Gratt (Va.) 78; Ogden Board of Education *v.* Brown, 12 Utah 251.

[25] Schultes *v.* Eberly, 82 Ala. 242. Under the constitution of Alabama, the legislature cannot delegate the power of taxation to any corporation which is not municipal.

[26] McCabe *v.* Carpenter 102 Cal. 469.

[27] Steward *v.* Jefferson, 3 Harr. (Del.) 335; People *v.* McAdams, 82 Ill. 356; Burgess *v.* Pue, 2 Gill (Md.) 254; Smith *v.* Board of Trustees of Robertsonville Graded School, 141 N. C. 143; Minsinger *v.* Rau, 236 Pa. 327; Wright *v.* House, 188 Ind. 247; Barrow *v.* Bradley, 190 Ky. 480.

[28] Hassett *v.* Carroll, 85 Conn. 23; Kuhn *v.* Board of Education, 175 Mich. 438; Crawford *v.* Klamath County School Dist. No. 7, 68 Ore. 388.

[29] Marion, etc., M. Ry. Co. *v.* Alexander, 64 P. 978, 63 Kan. 72.

[30] Board of Education *v.* Best, 51 Ohio St. 138.

[31] Board of Education *v.* Robinson, 81 Minn. 305.

To what extent may the power of taxation be delegated? We read in one case [32] that

> . . . when the legislature grants that high power to another tribunal, it can only be exercised in strict conformity to the terms in which the power is granted and a departure in any material part will be fatal to the attempt to exercise it,

and

> In the construction of any grant of taxing power to any county or district, the rule is that it should be construed with strictness, the presumption being that the legislature has granted in clear terms all it intended to grant.[33]

Inasmuch as the power of taxation is legislative, can it be delegated to executive and judicial branches or officers? Cooley [34] elucidates the principle in the following language:

> It is only the delegation of legislative power to a nonlegislative body or person that is objectionable. If the power delegated is a ministerial one it matters not that the delegation is to another branch of government (Mo. Pac. R. Co. *v.* Highway Imp. District No. 1, 143 Ark. 261). . . . There is a difference to making the law and giving effect to the law; the one is legislative, the other administrative. The legislature must prescribe the rule under which taxation may be laid; it must originate the authority under which, after due proceedings, the tax gatherer demands the contribution; but it need not prescribe all the details of action (Lillard *v.* Melton, 103 S. C. 10; Quinn *v.* Hester, 135 Tenn. 373; McCabe *v.* Carpenter, 102 Cal. 469).

Most decisions point to the fact that legislative power can be delegated only to legislative bodies or to the voters or taxable inhabitants of a locality and not to executive or ministerial officers. There are some opinions to the contrary; for example, in New York where the State Commissioner of Education is vested with judicial powers he may also be empowered, under certain conditions, to cause a tax to be levied.[35]

The principle is obvious that delegated power cannot be greater than the power at the source. School boards cannot

[32] Judge of Campbell County Court *v.* Taylor, 71 Ky. 206.

[33] State *v.* Houston & T. C. Ry. Co., 209 S. W. (Tex.) 820.

[34] Cooley, "Taxation," Vol. I, Par. 78.

[35] Steward *v.* Jefferson, 3 Harr. (Del.) 335; Burgess *v.* Pue, 2 Gill (Md.) II; Allison *v.* Corker, 67 N. J. L. 576; McCabe *v.* Carpenter, 102 Cal. 469; 243 N. Y. 204.

assume authority to levy taxes on property which the state itself cannot tax.[36] Neither can power be delegated to tax for other than public purposes. School boards cannot be vested with power to tax for other than public schools. The state, however, may delegate the power to tax property or subjects which could be taxed by the state but which, for reasons of public policy, are not taxed.[37] The following excerpt from a case in Virginia supports the argument: [38]

> When the legislature confers the general power of taxation, it grants all the powers possessed by itself in respect to the imposition of taxes; and a city can then impose taxes in its discretion upon all subjects within its jurisdiction not withheld from taxation by the legislature, whether they are taxed or not by the state.[39]

The courts are not in agreement on whether authority to tax is delegable to officers not elected by the people. In Iowa, Alabama, and North Dakota, for example, the power to tax cannot be delegated to nonelective boards or officers.[40] But in Minnesota, Maryland, and Indiana, as examples, the contrary view is maintained and appointive officers may acquire by delegation the power to tax.[41]

In most jurisdictions the imposition of a tax to provide school revenue must be made by a vote of the people at the annual meeting. In such case the meeting cannot delegate to the board of education discretionary power as to the amount of tax to be levied.[42] The people must vote the tax in a definite amount or the action of the board in submitting the levy will be invalid.

May the state recall power delegated to the school districts?

[36] Baldwin *v.* Montgomery, 53 Ala. 437; Walker *v.* City of Richmond, 173 Ky. 26; Lancaster *v.* Clayton, 86 Ky. 374; Townsend *v.* Smith, 144 Ga. 792; Livingston *v.* Albany, 41 Ga. 21; O'Donnell *v.* Bailey, 24 Miss. 368.

[37] Montgomery *v.* Knox, 64 Ala. 463; Canova *v.* Williams, 41 Fla. 509; Johnson *v.* Macon, 62 Ga. 645.

[38] City of Norfolk *v.* Norfolk Landmark Pub. Co., 95 Va. 564.

[39] *See also* McCabe *v.* Carpenter, 102 Cal. 469.

[40] State *v.* Des Moines, 103 Iowa 76; Vallelly *v.* Board of Park Commissioners, 16 N. D. 25; Schultes *v.* Eberly, 82 Ala. 242; Hinze *v.* People, 92 Ill. 406; People *v.* Detroit, 28 Mich. 228; Marr *v.* Euloe, 1 Yerg. (Tenn.) 452.

[41] State *v.* West Duluth Land Co., 75 Minn. 456; State *v.* District Court of Hennepin County, 33 Minn. 235; Baltimore *v.* State, 15 Md. 376; Burgess *v.* Pue, 2 Gill (Md.) II; School City of Marion *v.* Forrest, 168 Ind. 94.

[42] Trumbull *v.* White, 5 Hill (N. Y.) 46; Robinson v. Dodge, 18 Johnson (N. Y.) 35; San Francisco, etc., Co. *v.* State Board, 60 Cal. 12.

Since such power is not inherent in the district the state may at its will recall it. It thus becomes clear that whatever power the school district may possess is not of itself, but is subject to and derived from the state. This principle cannot be too strongly emphasized. When boards of education once fully realize that all their powers of taxation are derived from a higher authority, and that they must look to the express grant of power for its exercise, they will more carefully perform the functions entrusted to them and more frequently question the validity of their own acts when not supported by competent authority.

The Duty Imposed Upon the School Officers to Tax

Having discovered the authority through which and by means of which school board officers acquire and exercise their powers of taxation, a further question presents itself. Does such delegated power become a duty? In other words, must the officers of a school district exercise the power of taxation even though they or their electors may object to such exercise?

It does not require a great amount of reasoning to reach the conclusion that the state's function of providing a uniform system of education and equal educational opportunities for its future citizens cannot be performed unless the state reserves the power to compel the local school subdivisions to support the schools by means of adequate funds derived from taxation. No less eminent an authority than Judge Cooley [43] pronounces the dictum that "the state reserves to itself the means of giving complete effect to laws establishing the public school system, even though a majority of the people of a district, deficient in proper appreciation of its advantages, should refuse to take upon themselves the expense necessary to give them a participation in its benefits." He continues with the final conclusion [44] that "the legislature may compel local taxation for school purposes" and cites abundant proof for the conclusion.[45] One of

[43] Cooley, *Taxation*, Vol. I, Par. 422.

[44] *Ibid.*

[45] Revell *v.* City of Annapolis, 81 Md. 1: Board of Education of City of Kingfisher *v.* City of Kingfisher, 5 Okla. 82; Atchison, T. & S. F. R. Co. *v.* State, 28 Okla. 94; State *ex rel* Clark *v.* Haworth, 122 Ind. 462; *Same v.* School Dist. No. 99 of Neosha County, 71 Kan. 843; Southern Ry. Co. *v.* St. Clair County, 124 Ala. 491.

the cases to which Judge Cooley refers and one famous for its elucidation of the principle in question is that of Revell *v.* City of Annapolis. We can do no better than repeat the exact words of Chief Justice Robinson, who presented the opinion of the court:

> . . . the legislature has the power to provide for the erection of a public school building in the city of Annapolis, and to direct that the city authorities shall issue bonds for the purpose of raising money to pay the cost of such building, and this too with or without the consent of the voters of said city. . . . All the cases agree that a municipal corporation cannot be compelled to incur a debt for a private purpose and in some cases it has been decided that it cannot be compelled to create a debt for a local purpose in which the state has no concern. . . . We have been unable, however, to find a case which denies to the legislature the power to compel a municipal corporation to incur a debt for the purpose of erecting a public school building within the city limits for the use of public schools. Such an object being a *public object,* and one strictly within the functions of municipal government, there is no ground on which the exercise of such a power can be denied.

Other cases fortify the same conclusion, among them Southern Ry. Co. *v.* St. Clair County, Alabama,[46] wherein a tax imposed by authority of the legislature for the better support of schools was upheld though it was for a local purpose. The current of judicial opinions which supports the conclusion that it is for the legislature to decide whether it shall exercise the authority to tax directly or whether that authority shall be distributed to a county, a township, or a district organization is unbroken.[47] When school officials and taxpayers hesitate to provide the funds which the sovereign power deems necessary to carry into effect its educational purposes, then the legislature commands that its will be done in direct fashion over the dissent of the locality.

The foregoing principle is far different from the one involving the withholding of the taxing power from a subdivision. It seems that if the power of taxation must come from the state, that same authority might at its pleasure withhold the grant

[46] 124 Ala. 491.

[47] Clark *v.* Haworth, 122 Ind. 462; State *v.* Board, etc., 35 Ohio St. 368; School Commissioners *v.* State Board, 26 Md. 505; Robinson *v.* Howard, 84 N. C. 151; Stuart *v.* School Dist. No. 1, 30 Mich. 69; Ford *v.* Kendall Borough School Dist., 121 Pa. St. 543; People *v.* Board, etc., 101 Ill. 308; Richards *v.* Raymond, 92 Ill. 612; Rawson *v.* Spencer, 113 Miss. 40.

entirely. But in our plan of government there is a distinct place for local self-government and it is doubtful if any state lawmaking body has been intrusted with the power to abolish the local government without substituting another in its place. Such a conclusion is absolutely sound with respect to municipal governments. But education is not a purely local matter and it has been shown that the state may adopt any method it pleases to effectuate the means of exercising that function. If necessary it may remove local taxation entirely; that is, taxation through the agency of the school district, and substitute therefor state taxation on the subjects and property within the district,[48] in order to support schools.

The Police Power Versus the Taxing Power

> The police power is of great and growing legal importance in the United States, largely because of the peculiar principles of American governmental relations, whereby local bodies are deemed to have only those powers expressly delegated to them, in contra-distinction to the European method according to which local bodies possess in certain respects all powers not expressly forbidden to them. The courts, therefore, have been compelled to uphold much under the police power that under other and more favorable conditions they would have upheld under the taxing power.[49]

There is a distinction between the police and the taxing power which school administrators should recognize. The taxing power is employed for raising revenue and is subject to constitutional limitations. The police power is exercised for promoting the general welfare and its object is regulation and not revenue. It is not subject to the restrictions surrounding the power of taxation.[50] When a license is demanded as a prerequisite to engaging in business, erecting new buildings, and the like, the police power is invoked, and not the taxing power. While this power may be delegated to subordinate boards and to municipalities, but not to individuals, boards of education are not commonly intrusted with it. Even if the board of education

[48] *Ante,* footnotes 1, 5, 47.

[49] Seligman, E. R. A. *Essays in Taxation,* p. 404.

[50] *American and English Encyclopedia of Law,* Vol. 22, 917; Walker *v.* Jameson, 140 Ind. 591; Carthage *v.* Rhodes, 101 Mo. 175; St. Louis *v.* Know, 6 Mo. App. 247; State *v.* Hoboken, 33 N. J. L. 280; Charleston *v.* Werner, 38 S. C. 488.

should be intrusted with police power in such matters as health regulations, there is no collateral power of deriving any of the funds raised from fees therefrom. Consequently, no supplementary revenue may be procurable by boards of education through delegated police power; indirectly, however, licenses, fees, and occupation taxes may find their way into the public school funds. But the control of such funds is entirely outside the power of boards of education.

Purposes for Which Taxes May Be Levied

It is a settled principle of constitutional law, fortified and supported by a long and unbroken series of decisions by the courts of last resort, that taxes can be levied only for public purposes. More recent decisions [51] only add to the strength of the principle laid down by earlier decisions.[52]

But it has not been so easy to define what a public purpose is, and changed conditions may render nonpublic a purpose which was once public, or public, purposes which were private. The term "public purposes" as generally employed is merely a classification to distinguish objects for which, according to usage, the government provides.[53] With the increase of governmental functions brought about by expansion of state and national governmental activities, purposes not long since deemed private are now objects for which taxes are being levied. Since the decision as to whether a tax or a debt is for a public or a private purpose is not a legislative but a judicial function, courts are continually being called upon to make their declaration on such a question.

It is certain that taxes for public education are for a public purpose. Were this study not considering the legal limitations on the powers of the boards of education with respect to taxation, that is as far as it would need to go. But boards of education are taxing bodies or represent the people of their district in this respect and should be fully cognizant of the

[51] City of Tombstone *v.* Marcia, 245 P. 677; State *v.* City of Wilmington, 134 A. 694.

[52] Citizens' Saving, etc., Association *v.* Topeka, 20 Wall 655; Beach *v.* Bradstreet, 85 Conn. 344; Board of Education *v.* Blodgett, 155 Ill. 441.

[53] People *v.* Township Board of Salem, 20 Mich. 452.

limitations surrounding this power. When we speak of public education we mean not only the public common schools but also high schools,[54] state colleges and universities,[55] normal colleges and agricultural colleges;[56] in fact, all institutions controlled in whole or in part by the state.

But boards of trustees of private institutions have no right to invoke the use of taxation for their support. While in a few states the practice of giving assistance to privately owned schools out of the public purse has prevailed, this right has received little attention in the courts. Where such appropriations have been made, it is clearly settled that they must be for some strictly public purpose, such as carrying out part of the state's educational scheme through agencies not purely public. The appropriation is not to the agency but to the object which it serves for the state. It must be clearly understood that the state, not the school district, can make such appropriations.[57] The general rule among most of the states is that taxation for private schools is unconstitutional and inimical to public policy. Many states by constitutional prohibition forbid appropriation of public money in aid of sectarian schools [58] and in some of the states the prohibition extends to private institutions.

Since this study is more concerned with the court constructions relative to statutory enactments, let us examine an outstanding case or two to discover a declaration of principle on this point. In Jenkins *v.* Inhabitants of Andover,[59] it was decided that a town has no authority to raise by taxation and appropriate money to support a school as a public school which is founded by a charitable bequest that vests the order and superintendence of it in trustees, who, though a majority of them are to be chosen by the inhabitants of the town, yet are

[54] State *v.* Freeman, 61 Kan. 90; Southern Ry. Co. *v.* St. Clair County, 124 Ala. 491.

[55] Marks *v.* Trustees of Purdue University, 37 Ind. 155; Higgins *v.* Prater, 91 Ky. 6; People *v.* Auditor General, 19 Mich. 13; James *v.* State University, 131 Ky. 156; Sinclair *v.* City of Lincoln, 101 Neb. 163.

[56] Boehm *v.* Hertz, 182 Ill. 154; Rutgers College *v.* Morgan, 70 N. J. L. 460.

[57] Hager *v.* Ky. Children's Home Soc., 119 Ky. 235; City of Minneapolis *v.* Janney, 86 Minn. 111; Wis. Indus. School for Girls *v.* Clark County, 103 Wis. 651.

[58] Cal., Colo., Del., Fla., Idaho, Ill., Kan., La., Mass., Miss., Minn., Mont., Nev., N.J., Pa., S. Car., S. Dak., Texas, Utah, Va., Wyo.

[59] 103 Mass. 94.

limited to members of certain religious societies. Chief Justice Dixon in Curtis *v.* Whipple [60] used strong language in condemning the attempt to support a private school by means of taxation because it was contended that the institution was a benefit to the locality. He said in part:

> It can no more be supported by taxation than if it were incorporated. . . . Nor will the location of the institution at Jefferson, and the incidental benefits which may thereby arise to the people of town, sustain the tax. That is not the kind of public benefit and interest which will authorize a resort to the power of taxation. Such benefits accrue to the people of all communities from the exercise of any trade and employment, and the argument, pursued to its logical result, would prove that compulsory taxation might be made use of for the purpose of building up and sustaining every such trade or employment.

It has been held [61] that funds may be raised by taxation to pay tuition for pupils from one school who are sent to another district, but all tuition pupils must be *bona fide* and perfectly entitled to attend another school at the expense of their home district. Another decision,[62] however, permitted the issuance of an injunction against a school board's expending school funds to transport children from outside the district between schools for school contests, and to transport teachers to conventions. Boards of education are fully within their rights in providing through taxation funds for every school purpose so long as they keep within the statutory limit of taxation and do not expend the funds for purposes considered dissociated with public education. As an example of such extraneous purpose, we may mention the raising of funds by taxation to pay debts incurred in aid of a railroad or highway or any other business enterprise. An interesting case of a school district incurring a debt to aid a railroad is that of Weightman *v.* Clark.[63] A congressional township in Illinois, by law merely a corporation for school purposes, by a vote of the people, subscribed for bonds of a railroad passing through the township. After several years'

[60] 24 Wis. 350.

[61] Associated Schools of Indep. School Dist. No. 63 *v.* School Dist. No. 83 of Renville County, 142 N. W. (Minn.) 325.

[62] Schmidt *v.* Blair, 213 N. W. (Iowa) 593.

[63] Weightman *v.* Clark, 103 U. S. 256; People *v.* Trustees of Schools, 78 Ill. 136; People *v.* Dupuyt, 71 Ill. 651; Trustees *v.* Railway Co., 63 Ill. 299.

interest had been paid, a taxpayer brought suit to enjoin further taxation to meet the bonds. Chief Justice Waite, delivering the opinion of the court, said in part:

> A railroad may help the people in a school district, but it can hardly be said that the construction of a railroad is a school purpose. . . . The construction of railroads is not necessary either to the establishment or maintenance of schools.

The Amount of Tax That May Be Raised

Although one important phase of the amount of taxes will be more fully discussed in a succeeding chapter,[64] a complete outline of the nature of the taxing power would not be complete without including the general principles underlying it. Several questions wait for answers in this connection:

What limitations exist on the amount of taxes?

What authority imposes these limitations?

May school boards include the cost of loss and collection in raising funds for school purposes?

Does the amount of bonded indebtedness affect the amount to be raised for current expenses?

In the absence of constitutional or statutory provisions there is no limit upon the rate or amount of taxes that may be raised for school purposes. In Christopher *v.* Robinson[65] it was held that the voters of a district might vote one tax after another until a sufficient sum was raised to conduct the school according to their notion. But in most jurisdictions, there are provisions in the constitution or on the statute books limiting the amount of taxes that may be raised for school purposes in any one year. Usually this limitation is confined to a certain rate on taxable property. The legislative authority of the commonwealth imposes this limitation in the absence of express provisions in the constitutions. The principle that the legislative body may impose or cause to be imposed any amount of taxes it sees fit is an old one in our scheme of government. Taxation may be employed even to the point of destruction of property taxed,

[64] *See* Chapter V, "Levy in Excess of Statutory Limit."

[65] 164 Ky. 262.

which rule is well defined in the noted McCulloch case[66] wherein Chief Justice Marshall pronounced the opinion of the court. Where limitations are prescribed, boards of education are required to keep within them in every respect and can go beyond such limitation only with the express sanction of legislative enactment.

Boards of education may include the cost of and the loss due to collection of the tax in their estimated amount, if reasonable, according to some rulings,[67] but cannot do so if the levy, including these costs, will exceed the statutory limit. A limitation on the amount of bonded indebtedness in a school district is no limitation on the power of the district to levy taxes, as the mere levying of taxes is not the incurring of indebtedness. Taxes for current expenses may still be levied after the limit of bonded indebtedness has been reached.[68] Where high school districts and common school districts are coterminous but are managed by separate boards, there is much conflict of opinion as to whether the limit placed upon the amount of taxes refers to each separate district or to both of them combined.[69] If the law of the particular state is not clear on this point, it remains for the courts to interpret it in the light of what the legislature intended under varying conditions in that jurisdiction.

Uniformity and Equality of the Tax

Although equality and uniformity of taxation are matters with which the legislature is primarily concerned, school officers should have a knowledge of what the terms imply in the general scheme of taxation. The two terms "equality" and "uniformity" have particular reference to the following: tax rate, assessment, valuation of property, territorial uniformity, and procedure to assess and collect the taxes. Subject to provisions in the Federal

[66] McCulloch *v.* Maryland, 4 Wheat (U. S.) 316.

[67] People *v.* N. J. Sandberg Co., 118 N. E. (Ill.) 469; People *v.* Klee, 118 N. E. (Ill.) 754; *see also* Chap. VII, "Disposition of Proceeds of the Tax," subtopic, "Salaries and Commissions of Collector."

[68] Cincinnati, L. & C. Ry. Co. *v.* People, 206 Ill. 387; People *v.* Illinois Central R. Co., 309 Ill. 277.

[69] People *v.* Chicago & I. M. Ry. Co., 100 N. E. (Ill.) 174; People *v.* Henkle, 100 N. E. (Ill.) 175; People *v.* Hassler, 104 N. E. (Ill.) 177; Crabb *v.* Celeste Indep. School Dist., 132 S. W. (Tex.) 890, judgment modified, 146 S. W. 528; Marion & M. Ry. Co. *v.* Alexander, 64 P. 978; People *v.* Read, 233 Ill. 351.

Constitution forbidding discrimination between persons or property of the same class, taxation does not have to be equal or uniform in a commonwealth unless required by its constitution. However, if all the same class and property of the same kind are not taxed alike, taxes are invalid regardless of the state constitution because of violation of the federal provisions.[70] In all but three of the state constitutions [71] there are provisions requiring equality and uniformity.

Absolute equality and uniformity are impossible and are not required because unattainable.[72] The principle followed in the matter is that practical equality and uniformity under present conditions is what the lawmaking body intends. To tax property of the same kind or people in the same class at different rates renders such tax unequal and uniform. Different methods of taxation are not inconsistent with uniformity and equality. So far as school districts are concerned, equality of taxation does not mean that equal benefits shall accrue to each taxpayer according to the amount of tax he pays. So long as a taxpayer has taxable property in the district, he cannot refuse to pay his proportionate share of the school burden on the grounds that he receives less benefit than others.[73] To invoke an equal benefits rule would jeopardize the whole scheme of taxation.

One important aspect of this requirement of significance to those who have the responsibility of levying taxes for the schools is that the tax must be uniform over the territory affected. The principle is clearly enunciated by Justice Gantt in Turner *v.* Althaus: [74]

> Now the sum of the whole matter is, that all the property of a city or rather of a tax district, constitutes its wealth, and the cardinal principle in the imposition of taxes is, that they should be apportioned among all the citizens of the district according to the value of their respective properties . . . and upon this power to assess and tax the individual

[70] Campbell County *v.* Newport, 174 Ky. 712.

[71] Connecticut, New York, and South Dakota (eliminated by amendment in 1918).

[72] Gafill *v.* Bracken, 145 N. E. (Ind.) 312; Anaconda Mining Co. *v.* Junod, 227 P. (Mont.) 1001; First National Bank *v.* Chapman, 173 U. S. 205; Norwood *v.* Baker, 172 U. S. 269; Comer *v.* Folsom, 13 Minn. 219. For further authority *see* Cooley, "Taxation," Vol. I, p. 559.

[73] State *v.* Clement National Bank, 78A (Vt.) 944; *post,* Chap. III, note 34.

[74] 6 Neb. 54.

> property depends the very existence of the government and the maintenance of the orderly administration of its police power. . . . If property is to be differently and ununiformly taxed, who is to be the arbiter to define this line, and where is it to be exactly found?

The case arose over collection of taxes on property in the city of Omaha, not subdivided into lots and used for agricultural purposes. The owner contended that the tax rate should be reduced on this property because it was remote from the business district of the city and did not derive benefits in proportion to property more favorably situated. If such a rule obtained as this owner wished enforced, every tax district would be under the necessity of zoning all of its territory for the application of different tax rates. And as the eminent justice asks, who would be competent to locate equitably those zoning lines? The only relief for such a taxpayer is that of having the assessed valuation of his property reduced.

Summary

1. The school district or other local subdivision authorized to conduct the schools has no inherent power of taxation. It acquired such power only through delegation from the state legislature.
2. The extent of the legislature's power to tax and, therefore, to delegate the taxing power is unlimited except by the constitution.
3. The state, through its legislative body, may exercise the power of taxation over the locality to the extent of imposing taxation on the locality against its wish for the support of public schools.
4. Delegated power must be exercised in strict conformity to statutory enactments. This delegated power of taxation may be recalled at the will of the state.
5. Boards of education not only possess, through delegation, the power to tax, but are duty bound to exercise it, even though they or the taxpayers, deficient in appreciation of education's benefits, refuse to sanction the tax.
6. School taxes can be levied for all schools controlled in whole or in part by the state, but are generally forbidden for private

and religious schools, under the principle that all taxation must be for a public purpose.

7. The amount of tax as well as equality and uniformity of imposition are matters for the state to determine.

CHAPTER III

THE PERSONS AND THE PROPERTY THAT MAY BE TAXED AND THE PLACE OF TAXATION

Boards of education are responsible for providing funds with which to operate the schools in an efficient manner. Taxation is their only source of revenue. It is therefore incumbent upon them to possess a knowledge of their rights and liabilities with respect to the persons and the property taxable in their district. Although the board itself may not be responsible for the assessment and the collection of taxes, such a fact does not relieve it of the obligation to be certain that all taxable persons and property are furnishing their proportionate share of the public school burden. To permit some persons or property to escape a just share in the support of the schools only increases the burden upon others.

Ordinarily, the same principles regarding persons and property taxable for school purposes as for other governmental purposes govern. In fact, so far as its political subdivisions are concerned, the state does not designate that certain persons and property shall be taxable for county purposes, others for municipal purposes, and still others for school purposes. Many states, by statute, prescribe the property which is taxable for each governmental purpose and property not so indicated is generally held to be nontaxable, while other states provide that all property not expressly exempted by statute is taxable.

Persons Who Are Taxable

In the category of persons liable to taxation no one is omitted if he owns property subject to tax within the jurisdiction of the taxing district.[1] Not even are infants,[2] insane people,[3] or aliens [4]

[1] Wheeler *v.* Wall, 6 Allen (Mass.) 558; Finley *v.* Philadelphia, 32 Pa. St. 381.

[2] Payson *v.* Tufts, 13 Mass. 493.

[3] Whitaker *v.* Ellis, 102 Wash. 43.

[4] Witherspoon *v.* Duncan, 4 Wall. (U. S.) 210; Mager *v.* Grima, 8 How. (U. S.); People *v.* Naglee, 1 Cal. 232.

excluded, since their property enjoys the protection of the law and the benefits of an educated community as much as does that of every other person. But many complications arise over persons and property under abnormal conditions.

An attempt will be made in the succeeding paragraphs to answer such questions as:

Is a resident of the district taxable therein on his property located in another district or outside the state?

Is property of a nonresident taxable to him where the property is situated or where he lives?

Are people temporarily located within a district taxable therein?

Is property temporarily within a district taxable there? If not, where is it taxable, at place of origin or place of destination?

Where is property to be taxed which is in more than one district?

What effect on taxability has transfer of property from one district to another?

What constitutes domicile?

May property have two taxable locations? If so, which one is controlling?

If a person has two residences, which one determines his taxable domicile?

May a person change residence purposely to escape taxation in a particular taxing district?

Classification of Taxable Property

For purposes of taxation property is generally separated into three categories: (1) real property (real estate), (2) tangible personal property, and (3) intangible personal property. It is obvious that real property can have but one situs,[5] namely, where it actually is situated. But even with this evident fact, there are complications arising under certain conditions which will be discussed later. But real estate, being immovable, is not subject to the inherent difficulties to which personal property is subject. Both from the nature of its mobility and the variety of taxing districts, personal property may have a twofold situs,

[5] Situs may be defined as location for a particular purpose.

one where it actually is and the other legislative or legal.[6] The legal situs is controlling if the statute is constitutional. But this must be held in mind: no legislative enactment can give legal situs to property where it and its owner are without the taxing state.[7]

> The power of taxation though an inherent attribute of sovereignty is limited to the taxation of persons, property, and business situated within the territorial jurisdiction of the state imposing the tax.[8]

The rule just quoted means that at least one of three things must exist: (1) the owner of the property must live in the taxing district, (2) the property must be located there, or (3) the business carried on with the property must be done within the taxing district.

Real Property of the Resident Citizen

Considered from the standpoint of the whole state, real estate is taxable in the state where located regardless of the residence of the owner.[9] This rule governs whether owner is citizen or alien. Land owned by the same person and in one body, but divided by a state line nevertheless is taxable in each state for the portion lying therein. Considered from the standpoint of taxing districts within the state, the same general rule applies that real property is taxable in the district in which it is located. This rule is entirely controlling when the property is wholly within the district. An excerpt from the ruling in a case [10] will support the discussion:

> We have not been able to find any case where any court has ever held, in the absence of an express statute authorizing it, that a municipality or school district had authority to levy a tax upon real estate outside of its limits. . . .[11]

[6] Hunt *v.* Turner, 45 So. 509; Chicago N. W. R. Co. *v.* State, 128 Wis. 553; De Ganay *v.* Lederer, 239 F. 568.

[7] Maxwell *v.* People, 189 Ill. 546; Endicott, Johnson & Co. *v.* Multnomah County, 190 P. (Ore.) 1109.

[8] *Supra,* note 7, 190 P. 1109.

[9] Savary *v.* Georgetown Fourth School Dist., 12 Metc. (Mass.) 178; Ryder *v.* Cudderback, 12 Johns (N. Y.) 412; Bronaugh *v.* Com., 188 Ky. 103; Stone *v.* New England Box Co., 216 Mass. 8.

[10] Chicago B. & Q. R. Co. *v.* Cass County, 51 Neb. 369.

[11] Hughes *v.* Ewing, 93 Cal. 414; *in re* Assessment of Chickasha Cotton Oil Co., 194 P. (Okla.) 215.

Citizens of a school district often own real property outside the district wherein they live. The question arises, where is such property taxable? If the property is not a part of the tract owned in the district of residence, but is a separate parcel, the rule laid down in Myer *v.* Crispell [12] is controlling in all cases. In this case a resident of school District No. 4 owned, improved, and operated another farm in school District No. 6. The lands were not contiguous. It was held that the tract in District No. 6 was properly taxable therein and not in District No. 4 where the owner resided. We deduce from this the principle that real property of the resident of a district located outside the district, separated from any land owned by the resident in the district, is taxable in the school district where actually situated. This principle reversed gives us the rule for the taxation of real property of a nonresident which is located within a school district. If separated from land owned by the nonresident outside the district, such property is taxable in the district where it is situated. And since it would invoke an unfair discrimination in favor of the person not a citizen to relieve his property of an equal share in the tax burden, aliens are taxed on the property they own which lies in the school district.[13]

A taxpayer who claims that his property is not in a certain school district must prove this fact.[14] And the fact that a person has sent his children to a certain school, has served as school trustee, and has been taxed therein does not prevent his denial that he is a resident of the district in order to defeat a school tax charged against him.[15]

Tangible Personal Property

THE RULE OF DOMICILE

Before it is possible to present an understandable discussion of the tax laws with reference to tangible and intangible personal property, it will be necessary to define the rule of domicile.

What is domicile? The term is not synonymous with residence as applied to situs for taxation. A person may have more

[12] 28 Barb. (N. Y.) 54; *also see* New Kirk *v. Same, Id.*
[13] *Supra,* note 4.
[14] Mills *v.* Thornton, 26 Ill. 300.
[15] Abney *v.* Bell, Ky. Law Rep. 443.

than one residence, but can legally have but one domicile.[16] A person's domicile constitutes his principal place of residence, his business, and his political relations. It connotes the fact of making the place a home for an indefinite period.[17] It is possible for a person to have his domicile in a particular locality without owning or even leasing property there, since he may live in a hotel or rooming house.[18] And again, it may be that a person has his domicile in one state, town, city, or school district, and his business office in another. To establish a domicile two things are necessary: (1) the intention to make the place one's home, and (2) the act of living there for an indefinite period. If a person lives in a place with the intent to remain there, it becomes his domicile and he cannot elect to pay taxes in another place.[19] But this question is not so easily disposed of since, when a person has two or more actual residences, contributory circumstances may enable him to select either one to be designated as his domicile. In a Kentucky case [20] it was held that the owner of a farm who lived thereon for several months of the year was taxable for personal property in the district where the farm was located although for the remainder of the year he lived in a neighboring city. The court stated in this case:

> Only one of these [residences] can be regarded as his residence for purposes of taxation, and generally that one will be treated as his permanent home to which, when absent, he intends to return.

The circumstances referred to in the previous citation may be similar to those in Agassiz *v.* Trefry [21] in which the complainant, domiciled in Massachusetts, also owned an individual interest in the former home of his deceased father in Rhode Island. By announcing his intention to change his domicile to Rhode Island, removing his securities there, going there on tax day in Massachusetts, and voting and paying his personal taxes there, but without any actual change of residence (his houses in Massachu-

[16] State *v.* Lench, 156 Wis. 631; Denny *v.* Sumner County (Tenn.), 184 S. W. 14.

[17] Holt *v.* Hender, 248 Ill. 288; Viles *v.* Waltham, 157 Mass. 542.

[18] *See* L. R. A., 1917 D, 388.

[19] Lyman *v.* Fiske, 17 Pick. 231; Dickinson *v.* Brookline, 181 Mass. 195.

[20] City of Winchester *v.* Van Meter, 164 S. W. (Ky.) 323.

[21] 266 F. 8; *see also* Stoddert *v.* Ward, 31 Md. 562.

setts being kept open and occupied, and his family being in Rhode Island only three weeks in the ensuing two years), it was held that he had not effected a *bona fide* change of domicile. Yet, if no circumstances intervene to overcome it, a person may change his residence with the expressed intention of escaping taxation on personal property in a certain district.[22] But this change of domicile must be accompanied by both act and intent. Nor does a person lose his domicile from a certain place until he has established it in another location. A domicile is not lost by absence on business or pleasure with the intent to return. It has been held that one who moves to town for the purpose of educating his children does not lose his original domicile if he intends to return to it when the education of his children has been completed.[23]

What is meant by the rule of domicile is that, in the absence of statutes fixing a different rule, the taxable location of all personal property is at the domicile of the owner.[24] How this rule under varying conditions is not controlling will be discussed under the following paragraph relating to tangible personalty.

TANGIBLE PERSONAL PROPERTY OF THE RESIDENT AND THE NONRESIDENT CITIZEN

The principle of *mobilia sequuntur personam* (movables follow the person) is a product of the Middle Ages when it was possible, and the only safe way for a person to carry his personal effects with him wherever he went. "The maxim is merely a legal fiction not allowed to be controlling in matters of taxation. It is subject to so many exceptions that it is liable to mislead when considered alone. So far as its application to taxation is concerned, it means that the situs of personal property is the domicile of the owner unless (1) there is a statute to the

[22] State *ex rel* Orr *v.* Buder, 271 S. W. (Mo.) 508; Draper *v.* Inhabitants of Hatfield, 124 Mass. 53; Lyman *v.* Fiske, 17 Pick. 231; Thayer *v.* Boston, 124 Mass. 132.

[23] Montgomery *v.* Lebanon, 111 Ky. 646; Denny *v.* Sumner County, 134 Tenn. 468.

[24] Hughes *v.* Ewing, 93 Cal. 414; Churchill *v.* Highland Park Graded School, 89 S. W. (Ky.) 122; Keneenaw Association *v.* Hancock Tp. School Dist. No. 1, 98 Mich. 437; Taylor *v.* Commonwealth, 98 S. E. (Va.) 5; Southern Ry. Co. *v.* Commonwealth, 264 S. W. (Ky.) 850.

contrary, (2) property is tangible and has acquired an actual situs of its own other than where the owner is domiciled, and (3) in case of intangible property it has acquired a business situs in a place other than the owner's domicile."[25] It is thus evident that personal property, especially that designated as tangible, may have a taxation situs different from the domicile of its owner. In Carmody *v.* Clayton[26] we have the principle that personal property which has its situs within the state is subject to taxation therein, regardless of the domicile of the owner. It is a well-recognized exception that, where the personalty has a business situs apart from the domicile of the owner, it is not taxable in the owner's domicile.[27] Thus it becomes clear that the personal property of a resident citizen may have a taxable situs either within the school district where he lives or without, depending upon whether such personalty is more or less permanently located within or without the district. In Bassett *v.* City of Boston,[28] office furniture and equipment required by a public accountant to carry on his business in the city of Boston, although he resided in the city of Newton, was taxable in Boston. In an Illinois case[29] where the defendant lived in Glencoe and maintained a law office in South Chicago, but did not make a return of his office fixtures in Chicago, it was held that he was not taxable in Chicago. These two cases settling the same issue in different rulings only proves the contention that personal property as a means of raising funds by taxation is objectionable in that it admits of so many interpretations of the various laws. But the principle that the taxable situs is where the property is more or less permanently located regardless of domicile is acquiring a wider application in this day of extensive corporations with property in many taxing districts.[30] The Supreme Court of the United States has now settled the prin-

[25] Cooley, "Taxation," par. 440. *See also* Endicott, Johnson & Co. *v.* Multnomah County, 190 P. (Or.) 1109; State Board of Assessors *v.* Comptoir, etc., 191 U. S. 388; Union Refrigerator Co. *v.* Lynch, 18 Utah 378.

[26] (Tex.) 154 S. W. 1067.

[27] State *v.* Harrington, 217 P. (Mont.) 681.

[28] 114 N. E. (Mass.) 1035.

[29] People *v.* Culver, 136 N. E. (Ill.) 682.

[30] Rockefeller *v.* O'Brien, 224 Fed. 541; Gallup *v.* Schmidt (Ind.), 54 N. E. 384; Clapp *v* Ward, 58 Mo. 296.

ciple that the state legislature cannot fix the situs of personal property, more or less permanently located in one state, at the domicile of the owner in another state.[31] All of the decisions bear out the conclusion that it matters not whether the property is that of a resident citizen, a nonresident citizen, or an alien. A recent Oregon decision [32] reads in part as follows:

> Where property is used in a business carried on in one state, and the owner of the property is domiciled in another state, the property used in that business becomes localized at the place where the business is conducted, and is taxable at that business situs.

With reference to taxing districts in a state, the same general principle is controlling as evidenced by the decision in a case in Alabama [33] where the resident of one county was taxed in another county for a portable sawmill which he had kept in the latter county for three years. The sawmill was considered more or less permanently located in the latter county.

Property Remote from the School Center

It frequently arises in the equalization of the tax burden that a taxpayer objects to the tax he is required to pay on the grounds of remoteness from the source of benefit. If this principle were allowed to control there would be no end to controversy over distances from schools as well as from other governmental benefits. The state may as well decrease state taxation in proportion to its remoteness from the state capitol as to permit property remote from a schoolhouse to be taxed less than property nearer to the schoolhouse. In a few states, the matter has come before the court of last resort with the anticipated opinion that the burden of taxation upon personal property within a school district does not depend upon the nearness to or remoteness from the schoolhouse.[34]

[31] *Supra,* note 30, 224 F. 541. *See also* Semple *v.* Commonwealth (Ky.), 205 S. W. 789; Trammell *v.* Connor, 91 Ala. 398; Mills *v.* Thornton, 26 Ill. 300; City of New Albany *v.* Meekin, 3 Ind. 481; Ewa Plantation Co. *v.* Wilder, 289 F. 664.

[32] Endicott, Johnson Co. *v.* Multnomah County, 190 P. 1109.

[33] Trammell *v.* Connor, 91 Ala. 398.

[34] (S. D.) Lebo *v.* Griffith, 173 N. W. 840. *See also* Turner *v.* Althaus, 6 Neb. 54; Carman *v.* Hickman County, 215 S. W. (Ky.) 408.

Intangible Personal Property

All personal property is subject to many objections as a source of revenue through taxation. But tangible personalty, being generally less easily concealed because of its corporeal nature, is not so objectionable as intangible property. Such intangibles as credits, bills receivable, bank deposits, bonds, and promissory notes are easily secreted and their discovery for taxation difficult. In the first place, such property cannot be assessed without an inquiry into the owner's private affairs, because most persons will not voluntarily return property for taxation. Second, there is the temptation to defraud the government by intentionally concealing such property. Thirdly, there is the possibility of duplication of taxation on the same property.

Legislatures have in many instances recognized these objections and have attempted to frame laws with the intention of removing them as far as possible. In the interpretations of those laws the courts have attempted in a highly intelligent manner to evolve principles of justice and equality. Necessarily there is considerable conflict of opinion among the courts of the various states. What few general principles are deducible will here be dealt with.

The first thing that must be borne in mind is that personal property of a nonresident located within the state is not taxable therein unless there is statutory authority therefor.[35] This is as true of tangible as of intangible property. Where the owner lives outside the taxing state, express and unequivocal words in the tax statute are necessary to make the property taxable in such state. And it is also settled that the state where the owner is domiciled has no power to tax it where the property has acquired an actual situs in another state. The United States Supreme Court has settled this question by holding that to do so violates the due process clause of the Federal Constitution.[36]

As has been shown above, it was long a general principle to

[35] Tobey *v.* Kin, 214 Mass. 477; Dallenger *v.* Rapello, 14 F. 32; Graham *v.* Tp. of St. Joseph, 67 Mich. 652; Commonwealth *v.* Sellinger, 30 Ky. L. Rep. 451; State *v.* Howard County Court, 69 Mo. 454; Berry *v.* Windham, 59 N. H. 288; Union Tanning Co. *v.* Com., 96 S. E. 780; Hall *v.* Miller, 110 S. W. 165.

[36] Union Refrigerator Transit Co. *v.* Kentucky, 199 U. S. 194; Westinghouse Electric & Mfg. Co. *v.* Los Angeles County, 205 P. (Cal.) 1096.

tax all personal property at the domicile of the owner. It soon became intolerable that a state could not tax tangible personalty permanently located within its boundaries, and a different ruling was given to taxation of such property. Then in the evolution of modern business less visible property, such as, stocks, bonds, notes, credits, and the like, became so common that they too have now become subject to somewhat the same principles of taxation as tangible property. The general rule is, however, when not provided otherwise by statute, that intangible property follows the domicile of its owner.[37] That this rule is still controlling, where no authority to the contrary exists, is the deducible principle from numerous decisions.[38]

But there are exceptions to the general rule which need to be noted. The legislature may provide otherwise than that intangible property should be taxed at the domicile of the owner. Particularly is this true with reference to certain incorporeal property employed in business. All the more reason has a state to pass laws for the taxation of such property if it exists in large quantities in the state but owned by nonresidents. Therefore, it is now well recognized that where property acquires a business situs apart from the domicile of the owner, it is taxable at the actual situs.[39] Frequently a particular business purpose cannot be served unless the intangible elements which support it become permanently located at the place of business. Even the rule that situs of personalty, such as mortgages and mortgage notes, follows the domicile of the creditor is not of universal application, even as to a property tax and gives way to a statute fixing the situs for purposes of taxation.[40] And securities may have a business situs separate and apart from the domicile of their owner where they are used in or as capital invested in a busi-

[37] Gulf Refining Co. *v.* Tillinghast, 94 So. (La.) 418; Land Title and Trust Co. *v.* Tax Commission, 126 S. E. (S. C.) 189; Rhode Island Hospital Trust Co. *v.* Doughton, 121 S. E. (N. C.) 741; Travers *v.* Dickey, 222 P. (Okla.) 527; White Bros. Lbr. Co. *v.* Corp. Tax Appeal Board, 192 N. W. (Mich.) 570.

[38] State *v.* Shepherd, 218 Mo. 656; School Dist. *v.* Wickersham, 34 Mo. App. 340; Burroughs on "Taxation," pp. 40 and 215; Cooley, "Taxation," 369.

[39] State *v.* Harrington, 217 P. (Mont.) 681; Guaranty Life Ins. Co. of Houston *v.* City of Austin, 190 S. W. (Tex.) 189, affirming judgment 165 S. W. 53; Scollard *v.* American Felt Co., 194 Mass. 127; State *v.* Packard, 168 N. W. (N. D.) 673.

[40] Helser *v.* State, 128 Md. 228.

ness, or as an instrumentality of such business; but such situs exists only by legislative action.[41] Bank deposits may be taxed at the domicile of the owner in some states or where they have acquired a business situs, or where they are actually kept, although the latter rule does not preclude their taxation in the state of the depositor's domicile.[42]

Property in More Than One School District

The general rule with respect to real property, as previously stated, makes all real property wholly within a taxing district taxable therein. But there is much landed property in the same tract, owned by the same individual, which is divided by the line separating two or more school districts. It remains to formulate the principle of taxation with regard to such property. Laws pertaining thereto are not in agreement, and a long series of legal decisions reveals different practices in the different states. As between states, the rule has been laid down that the portion of territory lying in each is taxable therein. But when we consider the tax subdivisions within the state there is much diversity of controlling principles.

The most general and precise rule that can be deduced is that, in the absence of any contrary legislation, land divided by the boundary of one or more districts must be taxed in each district upon the portion situated therein,[43] and a school district, therefore, cannot tax that part lying beyond its boundaries. But, in some jurisdictions, it is provided by statute that property lying partly in one district and partly in another and owned by the same individual is taxable for school purposes in the one where the owner resides.[44] In others, notably Pennsylvania, the property is returnable for taxes in the district wherein the mansion house is located.[45]

[41] Great Southern Life Ins. Co. *v.* City of Austin, 243 S. W. (Tex.) 778, reversing judgment, 211 S. W. 482.

[42] *Ibid.*

[43] Shaw *v.* Lockett, 14 Colo. App. 413; Arthur *v.* Polk Borough School Dist., 164 Pa. St. 410; Barger's Lessee *v.* Jackson, 9 Ham. (Ohio) 163.

[44] Budd *v.* Allen, 69 Hun. (N. Y.) 535; Judkins *v.* Reed, 48 Me. 386; Potter *v.* City of Orange, 62 N. J. L. 192; Tebo *v.* City of Brooklyn, 134 N. Y. 341; Jasper County *v.* Butts County, 142 Ga. 576.

[45] Arthur *v.* Polk Borough School Dist., 164 Pa. St. 410; Commonwealth *v.* Knoble, 88 Pa. Super. Ct. 562; Bausman *v.* Lancaster County, 50 Pa. (14

The case of Follett *v.* Butler County [46] reveals the situation with respect to Pennsylvania decisions in that the general rule is that the property divided by boundary lines is taxable where the mansion house is situated, but a slightly different division evokes a different ruling. Where a farm is divided by a township and a borough line, the land in the township is taxable therein and the land in the borough is taxable in it. The general rule seems only to apply when the school districts are of the same type. In the same state it was held [47] that where an owner of a farm divided by township lines built a new dwelling across the township line from his old dwelling and removed his family thereto, the whole farm became taxable in the township where the new dwelling was built. In Georgia, where a plantation was located across a county line it was returnable for taxation in the county where most of the improvements were.[48] In West Virginia [49] a village lot lying partly in one district and partly in another may be assesssed for taxation in the district in which the greater part in value lies. It has also been held [50] that where the real estate on which a manufacturing or business enterprise is conducted lies on or across a county line, the real estate is taxable in the county wherein the main buildings containing the machinery or most of such buildings are located.

Thus far the property in question has been lands extending into two or more school districts. What rule prevails if the house of a taxpayer is divided by a district line? The core of a Massachusetts' opinion [51] aptly furnishes the applicable principle, stating that where a dwelling house is so divided by boundary line between two towns as to leave that portion of the house in which the occupant mainly and substantially performs those offices which characterize his home (such as, sleeping, eating, sitting, receiving visitors) in one town, he is a citizen

Wright) 208; Cosset *v.* Reinhardt, 31 N. J. L. 218; Follett *v.* Butler County, 219 Pa. 509.

[46] *Supra*, note 45.

[47] Quigley *v.* Reiff, 39 Pa. Super. Ct. 425.

[48] Adams *v.* Floyd, 142 Ga. 607.

[49] Fleming *v.* Charnock, 66 W. Va. 50.

[50] Shoals Mfg. Co. *v.* Penick, 127 Ga. 504.

[51] Chenery *v.* Inhabitants of Waltham, 62 Mass. 327. *See also* Judkins *v.* Reed, 48 Me. 386.

of that town and has no right to elect to reside and be taxed for his personal property in the other town.

The Effect of Change of Boundaries of the School District, and Transfer of Property from One District to Another

School district boundaries are subject to change. Property situated in one district may, by a change of boundary lines, be located in another. Furthermore, indistinct district boundaries cause controversies over landed property on or near the boundary lines. While some of the controversies have had to do with the settlement of the question where children should attend school, the greater part of the litigation has resulted from disputes over taxation. Legislatures have provided laws governing the creation of new districts, and change of boundaries of existing districts. But the large number of cases reaching the supreme courts of the different states is abundant evidence that such statutes are imperfectly written or that their provisions are entirely too general to cover any variety of difficulties arising under them.

As a general rule, the power to levy and assess taxes upon all the property within the boundaries of the district extends to property annexed from another district before the time the levy was made.[52] A long line of decisions supports this rule. Property upon which a tax levy has been imposed is still subject to the tax even if relocated in another school district by a change of boundaries after the levy has been made.[53] The reverse is true if the property is relocated before the levy is made. Referring both to real property and to personal property taken into a district by a change of boundaries and the validity of taxes thereon, Chief Justice Conner in a Texas[54] case sums up the argument as follows:

> An examination of the cases that we have been able to consider has convinced us that, in the absence of limiting provisions in the law, terri-

[52] Visalia Savings Bank *v.* Visalia, 153 Cal. 206; Phelps *v.* Peoria School Inspectors, 214 Ill. 30; Grout *v.* Illingsworth, 131 Iowa 281.

[53] Hughes *v.* Ewing, 93 Cal. 414; Union Indep. Dist. *v.* Cedar Rapids Indep. Dist., 62 Iowa 616; Dyer *v.* Rutland School Dist. No. 1, 61 Vt. 96.

[54] Megargel County Line Indep. School Dist. *v.* Blewett, 278 S.W. (Tex.) 516.

tory annexed to an independent school district at any time during the year, as provided by law, and thereafter an election is held for an entire district authorizing the tax for that year and all subsequent years, the school board or the municipal authorities may lawfully vote the tax, make the levy and assessment in accordance with the statute, and that a tax, so assessed and levied can be collected for that year.[55]

In Crabb *v.* Celeste Independent School District,[56] it was ruled that where there is a constitutional provision requiring consent by the electors, a tax properly voted by the taxpayers of a school district cannot be extended over territory added to the district after the vote was taken, without giving the taxpayers of such addition an opportunity to adopt or reject it in the manner prescribed by the constitution. But the situation is otherwise where no such constitutional provisions exist. In the event a school district embraces territory outside the limits of a city, and subsequently the city boundaries are extended to coincide with the district boundaries, but thereafter are again cut down, the territory thus excluded from the city boundaries continues to be subject to taxation to pay bonds issued by the school district as originally created.[57]

No amount of elasticity in the laws and no amount of variety in the decisions, however, permits property to escape its share of the tax burden in a school district when the taxes have become due. Even though a portion of a district is set off from the main district against the will of the patrons so separated, the accrued taxes on the separated portion are collectable by the original district.[58] This is true even if the separated portion becomes a part of one large tract owned by a resident of another district, and which ordinarily would be taxed *in toto* where the owner resides.

It must not be assumed, however, that the mere transfer of the tax from one district to another transfers the land. It frequently happens that school children and the school tax of cer-

[55] State *v.* Holliday, 9 Ohio S. and C. P. Dec. 738; Cadena *v.* Texas, 185 S. W. (Tex.) 367; Gerhardt *v.* Yorktown Indep. School Dist., 252 S. W. (Tex.) 197; Kuhn *v.* City of Yoakum, 257 S. W. 337; Tuberville *v.* Gowdy, 272 S. W. (Tex.) 559.

[56] 105 Tex. 194.

[57] Chambers *v.* Adair, 110 Ky. 942.

[58] Marsh *v.* Early, 169 N. C. 465; Trustees of Paintville Graded Free School Dist. *v.* Davis, 64 S. W. (Ky.) 438.

tain property owners are transferred for school purposes from one district to another. But the property still remains a part of the district in which it was situated before the transfer proceedings. Transfer of the land would require a change of boundary, which is accomplished by an entirely different proceeding.[59]

People and Property Temporarily in the School District and Property in Transit

The increase of modern transportation facilities and the free movement of people and property throughout the United States have greatly increased the amount and the value of property away from its ordinary taxable situs. To subject such property to taxation while in transit would create a large amount of injustice and necessitate a greatly increased force of tax officers to enforce the collection of the tax. The problem involves several questions:

1. Are persons temporarily within a state taxable therein under provisions taxing the inhabitants for school purposes?
2. Is property in transit taxable while in transit?
3. If not taxable in transit, where is it taxable. At place of origin, or destination, or both?
4. Where in a state is property which is constantly moving taxable?

The Supreme Court of the United States[60] has put at rest any and all questions about capitation tax on persons temporarily engaged in business in a state if the state chooses to impose such taxes on them together with its resident citizens. The case came to issue over the payment of a school tax imposed by the territory of Alaska on men employed by a salmon packing company who, though spending several months in Alaska, were hired and paid off in California. In the course of rendering the opinion, the court said:

> One who is in a territory for the purpose of carrying on a business during the season when such business is properly and usually carried on is subject to the tax within the district where the business is carried on.

[59] School Dist. No. 4 *v.* School Dist. No. 84 (Ark.) 124 S. W. 238.

[60] Alaska Packers Association *v.* Hedenskoy, 267 F. 154.

The decisions of the courts are in perfect harmony relative to the taxation of personal or commercial goods in transit or temporarily located in a taxing district. A few clauses from the decisions in a few states will readily indicate the agreement.

> It is a plain proposition that property in the course of transportation from one state to another . . . is not liable to taxation.[61]
>
> Personal property found in transit through, or temporarily within, a state other than that in which the owner resides, cannot be taxed in the state in which so found. . . .[62]
>
> Chattels . . . temporarily located within the state do not as a general proposition acquire a situs for taxation within such state.[63]

The United States Supreme Court has supported the decisions of the state courts in ruling that one state cannot levy a tax on property in commercial transit to another state or country as such taxation would be in violation of the provisions of the Interstate Commerce Commission Act.[64]

Where then is such property taxable? Personal property temporarily within a district is taxable at the domicile of its owner,[65] provided it is not shipped in for sale. A gas fishing boat which was part of the equipment of a fishing business was ruled to be assessable for taxes, not where it had been moored during the winter freeze, but in the district where the business was located. A portable sawmill was held to be taxable where the owner lived although it was located outside the district. Tobacco delivered to the warehouse of a selling corporation was held not taxable if delivered for a temporary purpose. Notes held by a bank in a state other than that of the domicile of the owner for purposes of collection do not acquire a business situs in the state where the bank is situated and, therefore, are not taxable there but at the residence of the owner.[66]

The chief question for the court to decide in matters of temporary location is, when does temporary situs become more or

[61] (Ill.) Burlington Lumber Co. *v.* Willitts, 118 Ill. 559.

[62] (Ind.) Standard Oil Co. *v.* Bachelor, 89 Ind. 1.

[63] (Ky.) Commonwealth *v.* Union Pac. R. Co., 283 S. W. 119.

[64] Ogilvie *v.* Crawford Co. (C. C.), Fed. 745.

[65] Commonwealth *v.* Clyde S.S. Co., 110 A. (Pa.) 532; Joiner *v.* Pennington, 143 Ga. 438; City of Paris *v.* Burley Tobacco Co., 154 Ky. 320; Greilick *v.* Traverse City, 231 Mich. 699.

[66] Hinckley *v.* San Diego County, 194 P. (Cal.) 77.

less permanent? The question is not easily answered. Generally speaking, if the property is awaiting transportation facilities to resume transit it is not subject to taxation.[67] But if stored for an indefinite period during transit, or if some part of the manufacturing process is continued, or if awaiting sale, it is subject to taxation.[68] Coal brought into the state and stored in large quantities for an indefinite period subject to orders for future use was held taxable in New Jersey. Likewise flour shipped from the Northwest to New York, unloaded for repacking and blending in New Jersey, was held subject to taxation in New Jersey. Thus we come to the conclusion that when once property has reached its destination for sale it is taxable if in evidence on the day of assessment or as provided by law.

If property to be transported is in existence in the district of its origin or manufacture at the time the tax levy and assessment are made, it becomes taxable at such a place although it may later reach its destination in time to be taxed in a different jurisdiction. In Spaulding Manufacturing Company *v.* Kendall,[69] personal property assessed in another state on January first of a given year and brought into the territory before March first in the same year is liable for taxes for that year in Oklahoma, and in the State of Washington it was held[70] that personal property shipped into the state for sale, and otherwise taxable, was not exempt because it had been taxed for the same year in the state of the seller's domicile, since the state was subjected to the burden of its protection.

Property continually moving from place to place in a state, being first in one school district and then another, is generally held to be taxable at the domicile of the owner or at the place of the principal business office. For this reason, such property is not usually subject to the school district tax, but is taxed by the state. Railroad rolling stock and highway bus equipment may be cited as examples of such property.

[67] Board of Commissioners of Brown County *v.* Standard Oil Co., 103 Ind. 302.

[68] Susquehanna Coal Co. *v.* Borough of South Amboy, 69 A. 454; McCutcheon *v.* Board of Equalization, 87 N. J. L. 370; State *v.* Maxwell Motor Co., 171 N. W. (Minn.) 566.

[69] 19 Okla. 345.

[70] Spaulding *v.* Adams County, 79 Wash. 193; *see also* Callender Navigation Co. *v.* Pomeroy, 61 Or. 343.

The Time at Which the Situs for Taxation Becomes Fixed

The time at which situs for taxation becomes fixed is in most jurisdictions regulated by statute. The time of year differs with different states, some taking January first, others March first, and others some equally convenient date. If the state legislature has not prescribed a definite date, the date of levy usually governs.[71] Although the legislature has plenary power to provide for taxation of property brought into the state after the tax date, this is not commonly done, and if not so provided, property entering after the tax date is not taxable.[72] But property taken from the state or district after the tax date is still subject to the imposed taxes.[73] In Savary *v.* School District No. 4,[74] it was held that an inhabitant who removes from the district before the district votes to raise money for school purposes is not liable to be taxed for that purpose, though he was a member of the district on the first day of May before the vote passed. And in Gout *v.* Illingsworth,[75] a taxpayer whose property was in the district at the time of levy, although he had had no opportunity to vote in the election for members of the school board, was liable for the tax. Suffrage qualifications and taxability of property are in no way dependent one upon the other.

A Nebraska case [76] illustrates the principle of taxing personal property on the tax date with particular reference to fixing of ownership. Unlaid sewer pipe in a city on the first day of April was subject to taxation against the person who placed it there in performing a contract for the installation of a sewer at a price fixed for the entire contract.

It must be remembered, however, that the principle applied to property in transit and in temporary situs must not be violated even though discovered on the tax date. To be taxable, the

[71] Gillmor *v.* Dale, 27 Utah 372; State *v.* Nickerson, 99 Neb. 517; Walker *v.* Miner, 32 Vt. 769.

[72] Wangler *v.* Black Hawk Co., 56 Iowa 384; White *v.* State, 51 Ga. 252.

[73] People *v.* Holladay, 25 Cal. 300; Warren *v.* Werner, 14 Wis. 366.

[74] 53 Mass. 178.

[75] 131 Iowa 281.

[76] Dunegan *v.* Jensen, 199 N. W. (Nebr.) 722; *see also in re* Chapin-Colglazier Construction Co., 199 N. W. (Nebr.) 724.

property must have an actual or a constructive situs within the district.[77]

Summary

1. Since taxation is the only source of public revenue for the schools, boards of education should be cognizant of what property is taxable and the place where it is taxable. In no other way can they be certain that all taxable property is furnishing its proportionate share of the tax burden.

2. Real property is taxable in the district where located, except
   a. Where lying in one body and owned by one person but in more than one district, it may be taxable in the district of the owner's residence or where the mansion house is located.

3. Property of a nonresident is taxable as follows:
   a. Real property where it is situated;
   b. Personal property that has acquired a permanent situs, where it is situated; and
   c. Personal property, not of permanent situs, at the place of the owner's domicile.

4. Property temporarily in the district or in transit through the district is not taxable until it acquires a situs therein.

5. Remoteness from the school center in a school district is immaterial to the equalization of the tax burden on property.

6. Property transferred from one district to another is taxable in the one where located when the tax was levied and assessed.

7. The taxable residence of a person having more than one place of abode is where he by intent and act sets up his domicile.

[77] McIntosh *v.* Advance-Rumley Thresher Co., 117 Okla. 248.

CHAPTER IV

PERSONS AND PROPERTY EXEMPT FROM TAXATION

The Research Report of the National Industrial Conference Board for 1923 [1] reveals the fact that in 1921 the extent of the value of property exempt from taxation in the United States had reached the appalling figure of fifty-four billions, or 19.6 per cent of the national wealth. This privilege of exemption has some basis in reason, as when property is exempt from taxation because it is already performing a public service, but more basis in long established custom passed down for centuries. The stigma attached to taxation in ancient times prevented the property of the rich and powerful from being taxed; hence it was exempt, the owner often performing some public service presumably in lieu of taxation. But "tax exemption is a form of privilege which modern society has seen fit to curtail." [2] When one-fifth of a nation's wealth is exempt, the remaining four-fifths must bear a heavier burden. Each one of the states has sovereign power to tax or not to tax property and among them will be found exemptions of practically every class of property. Over one hundred different species of property are exempt in the states taken as a whole, one state exempting some species that others do not, and taxing some that others exempt.

It appears from the foregoing that further curtailment of the exemption privilege should be the object of future legislation. But such a problem is entirely beyond the scope of this study. However impatient we may be to propose that certain classes of property now exempt from taxation should be placed on the tax rolls, we are not at liberty to offer such a proposal in the defined limitations of this study. The question for us here never is, Should the property be exempt or taxed? but Is it exempt or is it taxed, and if exempt, for what reasons and to what extent?

Boards of education of the public schools and boards of trus-

[1] *National Industrial Conference Board, Research Report* of 1923, 61.

[2] *Ibid.*, p. 58.

tees of other educational institutions should have some definite knowledge on property exemptions both from the standpoint of clearly keeping within the law with respect to the property for which they are responsible and to have command of the situation with respect to all property which should be furnishing its share of the public burden. If property is rightfully exempt, it cannot be required to contribute revenue in the shape of taxes; but if it is hiding from taxation under an assumed exemption, it may be compelled to contribute its share of public revenue, by resorting to the proper action. Judged from the number of cases where exemption has been resolved against institutions and property claiming exemption, there must be considerable property now claiming exemption which legally is not exempt. In other words, the exemption is resting merely upon a presumption.

There may be said to be two general classifications of exemptions: (1) The property left untaxed when the selection of taxable subjects and property is made by the sovereign power. Under this category it is evident that there must always be some exemptions, since it is not probable that every item of goods and rights will ever be taxed in any one jurisdiction. It seems unlikely that memorials to past achievement will ever be taxed; and trees and shrubbery for ornamental purposes by their very nature will not be taxed except under capricious or most unusual conditions. (2) The persons and property expressly exempt by some provisions of constitutional, legislative, charter, or contractual nature. It is this second category of exemptions which concerns the writer of this study.

In addition, according to whether the property may be relieved of only certain kinds of taxes or of all taxes, there may be another dichotomous classification. Frequently, a state will exempt certain classes of property from "local" taxation or from "state" taxation. Again, certain classes of property are exempt from the regular assessment of taxes upon condition that they return to the state in lieu thereof a stipulated per cent of their capital stock. Particularly is this true of banks, railroads, and other corporations. It has not seemed wise to carry this study into the greatly increased intricacies of this latter phase of the subject. Rather will this chapter be confined to property wholly exempt when coming completely within the exemption provisions.

The Source of the Power to Exempt

The power to prescribe what property shall be taxed implies the power to prescribe what property shall be exempt.[3] We have noted that the power to tax is a sovereign power inherent in the people and expressed in either the constitution or in the law-making body. We have also noted that the legislature may exercise this taxing power almost without limit provided it keeps within the provisions of the constitution. In like manner the legislature may exercise its power to exempt property.

Much depends upon whether the constitution of a state contains permissive or mandatory forms of exemption. If the constitution provides that the legislature "may" exempt certain classes of property, the provision is not self-executing, and whatever property is exempt must be by expressed legislative act. On the other hand, if the constitution reads that certain classes of property "shall" be exempt, such a provision is self-executing, and the lawmaking body is powerless to tax such property. Even where the constitution provides that certain property may be exempt from taxation, the legislature may impose a tax on it.[4] No state has the power to exempt property outside its jurisdiction, even though such property may be owned by its own citizens.[5] If the constitution of a state expressly exempts certain classes of property, it is beyond the power of the legislature to limit or restrict such exemption.[6] But if the constitution provides that the legislature may exempt it, it is clearly within the legislative power to exempt in full or in part[7] or, as before stated, not to exempt at all. Speaking of enlargement of the exemption, a Kansas[8] decision reads in part:

[3] Gibbons *v.* District of Columbia, 116 N. S. 404; Asplund *v.* Alarid, 219 P. (N. M.) 786.

[4] City of Portland *v.* Kozer, 217 P. (Or.) 833; Gibbons *v.* District of Columbia, 116 U. S. 404; People *v.* Woman's Home Missionary Society of M. E. Church, 135 N. E. (Ill.) 749.

[5] Bank of Commerce *v.* New York, 2 Black (U. S.) 620; Bellous Falls Power Co. v. Commonwealth, 222 Mass. 51.

[6] Ottawa University *v.* Stratton, 85 Kan. 246.

[7] Corporation Commission *v.* Oxford Seminary Construction Co., 160 N. C. 582.

[8] State *v.* Joslin, 227 P. (Kan.) 543.

The enlargement of these exemptions by the Legislature is not expressly forbidden and is upheld where the same condition is met, that is, where the property exempted benefits the public in a way different from other property, and the legislative power is not used in such a way as to introduce a system of taxation substantially different from that contemplated by the constitution.

It is also a settled principle that the legislature has no power to exempt property used only in part for the purpose defining the exemption nor for other purposes than the provision prescribes.[9] The series of decisions upholding the state's power to exempt is a long and continuous one, yet throughout there is a striking harmony of opinion. An earlier decision [10] reads in part:

. . . 'taxes shall be levied on such property as the legislature shall prescribe.' And this necessarily implies that they may exempt from taxation such property as they see fit.

While a more recent one [11] says:

The power of taxation is inherent in the state, and may generally be exercised through its Legislature . . . except in so far as limited by the Constitution, and the state likewise has the reciprocal power of exempting from taxation, except as limited by the constitution.

The source of the power to exempt may then be summed up as follows: Unless restrained by constitutional limitations, the legislature may exempt from taxation all kinds and classes of property so long as the exemptions are uniform and equal, but where constitutional provisions are mandatory they must be obeyed.[12] This means that he who would be certain of the provisions in his own state must first of all become familiar with the constitutional provisions. After this he should have a knowledge of the present controlling statutes.

Exemption Statutes Classified

Statutes in the different states vary as to the basis for exemption of property. They may be classified into the following groups: [13]

[9] Morris *v.* Royal Arch Masons, 68 Tex. 698.

[10] (1853) Attorney General *v.* Winnebago, etc., Road Co., 11 Wis. 35.

[11] (1924) Asplund *v.* Alarid, 219 P. (N. M.) 786.

[12] State *v.* Elba State Bank & Trust Co., 91 So. (Ala.) 917; Jefferson Branch Bank *v.* Skelly, 66 U. S. 436; Appeal of Butler, 73 Pa. 448.

[13] See Cooley, "Taxation," Vol. II, Chap. 13.

1. Those statutes prescribing that ownership of the property by a certain institution or class of people be the test;
2. Those statutes making the particular use of the property rather than ownership the test; and
3. Those making both ownership and use the test.

If the exemption is based solely on ownership of the property, it is possible that property may be owned by an exempt institution, such as a school, and not used for the same purposes as is the larger part of the property of such institution, and still be exempt from taxation. As an illustration, a church, under such conditions, might hold a residence in its name, deriving rents therefrom, and this residence would be exempt under a strict interpretation of the statute.[14] But on the other hand, if use is the test of exemption, an owner of property may permit its use for school or religious purposes, rent free, and the property would be exempt as devoted to religious or educational purposes.[15] If use determines the exemption, it is its present and not intended use which governs as illustrated by a typical decision on this subject: [16] "It is the use of the property at the time when the tax is assessed which determines whether it is exempt from taxation or not." Until such time as the property is put to the required use to warrant exemption, it is taxable. It must not be forgotten that there are many circumstances which will render a different decision necessary in matters of exemption and that all we are able to do here is to set down the general principles in as brief and concise a manner as possible.

More states make "use of the property for a definite purpose" the test for exemption than do those which make ownership the test. The nature of such provisions may be seen from the decisions in a few states:

In ascertaining whether property is exempt under the constitution or statutory provisions, the primary use of such property must be considered; the light of exemption being determined by its use.[17]

The language of the exemption clause refers not to the character of

[14] University of the South *v.* Skidmore, 3 Pickle (Tenn.) 155; Wey *v.* Salt Lake City, 35 Utah 504.

[15] Benevolent Association of Elks *v.* Wintersmith, 263 S. W. (Ky.) 670.

[16] Matter of Mary Immaculate School of Eagle Park, 188 N. Y. App. Div. 5.

[17] (Ill.) People *v.* Catholic Bishop of Chicago, 140 N. E. 520.

the corporation or association owning the property, but, regardless of the character of the owner to the direct and exclusive use of the property for public charity.[18]

No property is exempt because it is used for educational purposes unless it is exclusively so used. . . . Property used exclusively for educational purposes is exempt, whoever may own it, or whoever may use it.[19]

In Louisiana,[20] it was held that a building was not exempt when used for a school unless the owner runs the school, thus illustrating the ownership test in that state. As an illustration of both use and ownership or either being test, a New York [21] decision states that property may be exempt from taxation by reason of its ownership by a person or corporation or by reason of the nature of the property itself.

Since this study is essentially judicial in its nature, a classification of persons and property exempt from taxation will not be made. For such a classification the reader is referred to the National Industrial Conference Board.[22]

Delegation of the Power to Exempt

Having noted that the power to grant exemptions from taxation is a power of the state directly associated with the taxing power, it remains to be seen whether this power may be delegated. This can be answered in the affirmative, for the possession of the power confers the right to delegate it.[23] In a comparatively recent decision,[24] we have the principle respecting the delegation of the power to exempt to the effect that the legislature, having the power to tax when not restrained by the constitution, can confer that power in such measure as it pleases, and also the included power to exempt from taxation.

Only so far as a school district may be coterminous with and fiscally dependent upon a city government does this delegation of the exemption power have any bearing. Although locally assessed and collected, school taxes are generally considered

[18] (Ark.) Grand Lodge *v.* Taylor, 226 S. W. 129.
[19] (Kan.) St. Mary's College *v.* Crowl, 10 Kan. 442.
[20] Armand *v.* Dumas, 28 La. Ann. 403.
[21] People *v.* Cameron, 124 N. Y. S. 949.
[22] *Research Report No. 64,* 1923.
[23] Colton *v.* City of Montpelier, 71 Vt. 413.
[24] Caverly-Gould Co. *v.* Village of Springfield, 83 Vt. 396.

"state" taxes rather than local and the state's power of exemption therefore need not be delegated. No decisions bearing upon the delegation of the power to exempt have been found wherein a school district was granted the right to exempt property from taxation, although from the foregoing discussion it is obvious that the legislature has the authority to delegate that power. The school district is a peculiar political subdivision, existing for the sole purpose of carrying out the state's purposes in education, and therefore, as such a direct agency of the state, it shares the state's powers even though they are not directly delegated.

Construction of the Statutes Granting Exemption

Inasmuch as public educational institutions are recipients of the exemption privilege when they themselves are relieved from taxation and are directly concerned with the loss of revenue due to the exemption of other institutions, it becomes incumbent upon those who need to know the most about the matter how the statutes granting exemptions are construed by the courts. Upon the construction given the statutes has hung the fate of many an issue not only in taxation but also in every other action at law.

There are just two ways of construing a statute, "strictly" and "liberally." The former interprets the statute as it reads, presuming nothing, admitting of no implications, and disregarding in general the intention of the framers of the statute. It does not mean an unfair, unreasonable construction, however, but hews close to the exact wording of the statute. The latter construction is, as the term suggests, one wherein a greater liberality is indulged, and the intent of the framers is taken greatly into account.

Since taxation is the rule and exemption the exception, exemptions are not favored, and in construing laws exempting any citizen or class of property all doubts are resolved against exemption.[25] In a long line of decisions,[26] the principle of strict construction is favored with respect to exemptions of property

[25] Santa Rosa Infirmary *v.* City of San Antonio, 259 S. W. (Tex.) 926, reversing judgment 249 S. W. 498.

[26] Waller *v.* Hughes, 11 P. (Ariz.) 122; State *v.* Kittle, 105 S. E. (W. Va.) 775; Commonwealth *v.* Rodgers Co., 123 A. (Pa.) 855; Brown *v.* Protective Life Ins. Co., 188 Ala. 166; City of San Antonio *v.* Y. M. C. A., 285 S. W.

from taxation. Opinions from a few cases will indicate the plain and certain language employed upon the subject:

> A claim of exemption from taxation by virtue of a statute is construed *strictissimi juris*. It must rest upon language in regard to which there can be no doubt as to the meaning, and the exemption must be granted in terms too plain to be mistaken.[27]
>
> Exemptions from taxation should be expressed in unmistakable terms. They are not to be inferred or implied from doubtful or ambiguous language. The presumption is that all property is taxable.[28]
>
> The universal rule of construction is that exemptions from taxation, whether statutory or constitutional, are to be strictly construed against the exemption in favor of the right to tax; and no person or property is to be exempted, unless the intention . . . clearly appears. . . .[29]

While the courts in all instances have favored a strict construction of the exemption statutes when private property is concerned, and many even favor a strict construction for all property, there is a growing number of decisions in which a liberal construction is favored with respect to educational, charitable, and benevolent institutions. Even the strict constructionists believe that no violence should be done to the statute so as to destroy its purpose or place a bar to its effectuated intent. In regard to the more liberal construction, Justice Graves, in State *v.* Trustees of William Jewell College,[30] elegantly presents the issue:

> It is urged that exemption statutes are to be strictly construed. Generally speaking, such is the rule. But we take it from the cases that there has been a well-recognized exception to the rule. Perhaps a better wording would be to say that the courts have never been overanxious to apply the rule so as to impose burdens upon religious, scientific, literary, and educational institutions.

In State *v.* Fisk University,[31] further words to the same effect are used by the court:

(Tex.) 844; School of Domestic Arts and Science *v.* Carr, 322 Ill. 562; Town of Cascade *v.* Cascade County, (Mont.) 243 P. 806; Rich *v.* Douhgton, 35 S. E. (N. C.) 527); People *v.* Board of Assessors, 202 N. Y. S. 50; Northwest Auto Co. *v.* Hurlburt, 207 P. (Or.) 161; *in re* Y. M. C. A. Assessment, 182 N. W. (Neb.) 593.

[27] Philadelphia, etc., R. Co. *v.* Maryland, 10 How. 376; Chicago Theological Seminary *v.* Illinois, 118 N. E. 662.

[28] Morrill *v.* Bentley, 126 N. W. (Iowa) 155.

[29] State *v.* Elba Bank and Trust Co., 91 So. (Ala.) 917.

[30] 234 Mo. 299.

[31] 87 Tenn. 233.

But this, like all other rules of construction, is made to rest upon the intention of the legislature, and will not be allowed to defeat the will of the lawmaking branch of the government. To apply this strict construction to individuals, and to corporations for profit, is but to announce the judgment of the courts upon the intent of the legislature . . . the same strictness of construction will not be indulged where the exemption is to religious, scientific, literary, and educational institutions.

Exemption is Never Implied

The right to levy and collect taxes is a necessary incident of every government, essential to its very existence, and is never presumed to have been surrendered or abandoned, except by clear words, and for what is deemed at the time, by the lawmaking power, an adequate compensation. The surrender cannot be extended by implication.[32]

Such words summarize the principle that the exemption privilege must be expressly granted. An owner claiming exemption from taxation under a statute must show clearly that the property is exempt within constitutional or statutory provisions. Even for charitable, religious, and educational institutions there can be no implied exemption.[33] It was held in an Illinois case [34] that land leased by the city and used for playgrounds, not inclosed with or a part of school buildings or grounds, was not exempt from taxation as being used for school purposes. The decision shows the fine line drawn between an expressed and an implied exemption, the former of which governs. In Percival *v.* Thurston County,[35] Justice Gordon, quoting Cooley on taxation, says in regard to this matter:

'It is said that as taxation is the rule and exemption the exception, the intention to make an exception ought to be expressed in clear and unambiguous terms; and it cannot be taken to have been intended when the language of the statute on which it depends is doubtful or uncertain.'

The United States Supreme Court [36] early ruled on the matter to the effect that in the absence of an express exemption, the property of a corporation should no more be presumed to be

[32] Jones Mfg. Co. *v.* Commonwealth, 69 Pa. St. 137; *see also* Waller *v.* Hughes, 11 P. (Ariz.) 122; Jefferson Branch Bank *v.* Skelley, 66 U. S. 436.

[33] People *v.* Jessamine Withers Home, 143 N. E. (Ill.) 414; Petition of Fuller, 197 N. W. (Mich.) 552.

[34] People *v.* City of Chicago, 153 N. E. (Ill.) 725.

[35] Percival *v.* Thurston County, 14 Wash. 586.

[36] (1850) Philadelphia & W. R. Co. *v.* Maryland, 51 U. S. 376.

exempt from taxation than the property of individuals. These brief words on the subject leave it plainly evident that boards of education cannot exempt property not expressly granted the exemption privilege, nor should they allow other property to escape its share of the burden for school support under an implied exemption which in law does not exist.

Persons Generally Exempt from Taxation

Individuals who, on their own account and not because of the property they own, are exempt in some states include ministers and priests, widows, orphans, unmarried women above twenty-one years of age, aged and infirm people, deaf-mutes, the blind, the indigent, veterans, soldiers and sailors, Indians, and firemen. This may mean that they themselves are relieved of capitation taxes, or that they pay no income taxes or that certain forms of their property are not taxed. But, as a general rule, the real property of no person escapes taxation by exemption and seldom does the personal property. Federal employees pay no federal income tax, but cannot escape general taxation in the place where residing for employment even though not domiciled therein and not being privileged to participate in the making of the laws that govern them. Residents of the District of Columbia cannot escape taxation there on the grounds that they have no choice in the framing of the tax laws which govern them, as being taxation without representation.

The reason for exempting the blind, the indigent, the orphaned, is that the state usually cares for such unfortunate people anyway and a tax on them would necessitate granting them an allotment with which to pay taxes. Veterans are exempt on the grounds of having rendered a commensurate public service, thereby encouraging the rendition of a similar service when the need arises in the future.[37]

State and Federal Instrumentalities

Under the existing form of government in the United States whereby two separate sovereignties operate in the same territo-

[37] State *v.* Snyder, 212 P. (Wyo.) 771; *see also* Harkin *v.* Board of Commissioners of Niobrara County, 222 P. (Wyo.) 35.

rial limits, for one to have power to tax the agencies of the other would soon destroy the dual existence of those governments, the more powerful taxing the other out of existence. Hence under these principles

> It is well established on reason and authority that neither government can interfere with the functions, agencies, or instrumentalities of the other, and neither can levy a tax upon the property, officers, agencies, or instrumentalities as such of the other . . . and the principles above announced are so well established as to be regarded now as fundamental and elementary. Whenever it can be said that a tax levied by a state is a tax upon the property, etc., as such of the federal government, it is void. And the rule is identical where the federal government levies a tax upon the property, etc., as such of a state.[38]

This principle does not mean that a tax levied by one government may not eventually be borne by the other, but does mean that it must directly and immediately constitute a burden upon the latter's functions.

Within the state itself, the exemption of public property of the state, county, or municipality is a matter of public policy. The power to tax such property exists unless exempt by law. However, property is not exempt from taxation for school purposes in many states simply because it is exempt from general city or town or state taxes.[39] It is generally held that property of a municipal corporation to be exempt must be owned by the municipality even though playgrounds and police and fire department quarters.[40]

Public School Property

It is not necessary to dwell at length on the immunity from taxation of public school property. To tax it would merely result in the necessity of raising more funds by taxation to pay the taxes on such property. It has become a recognized rule of the law of taxation that governments, even if they possess the power, should not tax the agencies through which their functions are performed. The only gain to be derived from such taxation

[38] Grayburg Oil Co. *v.* State, 286 S. W. (Tex.) 489; *see also* United States *v.* Bean, 253 F. 1.

[39] South Bend *v.* Notre Dame Du Lac University, 69 Ind. 344; Conyngham School Dist. Appeal, 77 Pa. St. 265.

[40] People *v.* City of Chicago, 323 Ill. 68.

would be that accruing to certain minor subdivisions at the expense of others or of the state as a whole, a thing never contemplated or tolerated by our principles of government.

It is necessary in most jurisdictions that school property be under the immediate control of the board of education to be exempt from taxation. Property leased by a board of education in which to hold school but the title to which remains in the owner of the fee is subject to taxation.[41] With the rapidly expanding school program and the common necessity for temporarily leasing additional buildings for classrooms, boards of education should be cognizant of the fact that leased property is taxable and should not contract with the owner under the assumption that taxes are to be abated while the property is used for school purposes.

In like manner, property belonging to the school district when rented to another for purposes other than educational becomes subject to taxation, if taxing authorities see fit to enforce their rights. Frequently abandoned school buildings and excess acreages not used for school purposes are rented to others. Immediately they become taxable.

Colleges and Universities—What Property Exempt?

Since state normal schools and universities come within the same category as common and high schools, their property in general is exempt under the same conditions as the latter. Where those conditions are different, such as property of fraternities, residences of officers and teachers, they will be discussed in connection with privately endowed colleges, academies, and universities.

The statement that property of educational institutions is exempt from taxation is misleading. The layman at once assumes that all such property is exempt. If he were asked the following questions, what would his answers be?

Does ownership or use generally control the exemptions of such institutions?

What is meant by "educational purpose"?

[41] People *v.* Brooklyn Assessors, 32 Hun. 457; Pace *v.* Jefferson County Commissioners, 20 Ill. 644.

Is contiguous property used by the institution exempt? Non-contiguous?

Are residences of officers and teachers located on the campus exempt? Not located on or near the main campus?

Does incidental profit from tuition or use of property defeat the exemption?

Is property rented to others than those controlling the institution exempt?

Does the exemption extend to dormitories, fraternity houses, dining halls?

If part of the property is used for other than educational purposes, is the whole deprived of exemption?

Whether ownership or use governs the exemption of colleges, academies, seminaries, and the like, depends entirely upon the wording of the statute. If the statute reads that all property owned by such institutions is exempt, the use made of such property is not very material. Where such laws read that "all property used for religious, literary, scientific, and educational purposes," the ownership is immaterial. In many jurisdictions both ownership and use govern. In some states the statute reads that all "property used exclusively for school and religious purposes" shall be exempt. Under such a wording it was held that school property alone is not exempt.[42] In other words, where two uses are contemplated by the statute, one of them will not satisfy the requirement. As a general rule, it may be stated that use of property governs in more cases than does ownership. Property owned by such institutions but not used for the purposes of the institution is not commonly exempt.

The meaning of "educational purposes" is differently construed under different jurisdictions and under varying conditions, as will be seen later. The term as usually interpreted means all those purposes necessary to carry out the objects and perform the functions of the institution. Where the term "exclusively" is included in the law, there must necessarily be a stricter interpretation. A building used at the same time for a school and as a family residence by the person having charge of

[42] People *v.* Trustees of Northwestern College, 152 N. E. (Ill.) 555.

the school is not exempt unless the residential use is incidental thereto and regarded as a part of it.[43]

When use for strictly educational purposes is the test for exemption of an institution, those items of property not directly used for class and lecture rooms, libraries, study halls, and laboratories have caused a large amount of litigation in the various states to determine whether they too are exempt along with the regular buildings. It must not be supposed that the decisions are in perfect harmony.

Dormitories and Dining Halls. These are commonly exempt unless part of the building is used for an alien purpose, then the taxable part may be separated from the exempt.[44] The dormitories and dining halls do not have to be on the main campus if devoted to the same purpose as if they were on the campus;[45] nor does the fact that board and lodging are charged alter the exemption.

Residences of Officers and Instructors. The general rule is to exempt such buildings if located on or near the campus,[46] and if devoted exclusively to the purposes of the institution. Even the house occupied by a chef, a janitor, kitchen employees, and gardener, was held exempt when owned by the college, as were houses occupied by the chief engineer and the superintendent of buildings.[47] But residences rented by teachers for their own convenience although owned by a college have been declared taxable. There are contrary decisions on the residences of professors, particularly where the professor pays rent and has control of the residence, same being declared subject to taxation.[48] The home of the president of a college, located eleven blocks from the campus and not otherwise distinguishable from other dwellings, although owned by the college, and furnished to the

[43] Watson *v.* Cowles, 61 Neb. 216.

[44] Chicago *v.* Chicago University, 228 Ill. 605; Harvard College *v.* Cambridge, 175 Mass. 145; Yale University *v.* New Haven, 71 Conn. 316.

[45] State *v.* Carleton College, 191 N. W. (Minn.) 400.

[46] Griswold College *v.* State, 46 Iowa 275; State *v.* Carleton College, 191 N. W. (Minn.) 400; South Lancaster Academy *v.* Inhabitants of Lancaster, 139 N. E. (Mass.) 626; Kansas Wesleyan University *v.* Board of Commissioners, 120 Kan. 496; Ramsey County *v.* Macalester College, 51 Minn. 437; Phillips Academy *v.* Andover, 175 Mass. 118.

[47] Wheaton College *v.* Town of Norton, 122 N. E. (Mass.) 280.

[48] President, etc., of Williams College *v.* Assessors of Williamstown, 167 Mass. 505.

president as part of his compensation, was held subject to taxation in a recent decision.[49] These contrary decisions warn us that the general rule has many exceptions.

Contiguous Property Owned and Used by the Institution. Two recent decisions [50] have set forth the controlling principles regarding contiguous property in a clear and forceful manner. Both hold that all contiguous property reasonably necessary and devoted to the accomplishment of the purposes of the institution is exempt from taxation. This included, in one case, a 260-acre farm acquired to make an attractive setting for the college, to provide ample grounds for expansion, and to furnish farm produce for the college tables. In the other case, it included a demonstration farm, athletic fields, supply stores, and the chancellor's official residence. However, an 80-acre farm located two miles from the former college and not devoted to nor reasonably necessary for the accomplishment of the college's purposes was not exempt. Likewise, in another case [51] land used as a vegetable garden, the products of which were consumed by teachers and students, was not exempt. Nor was an athletic field acquired after a college had erected its buildings, separated from them by a street, accorded the exemption privilege.[52] But these exceptional cases are few and no doubt arise from the strict interpretation of a peculiarly worded statute from which there is no escape.

Effect of Incidental Profit of Exempt College. That a private school charges tuition does not deprive it of exemption on that account. The use of a small portion of the grounds of an exempt institution for a vegetable garden does not destroy the right to exemption of the whole, even if in some cases it does not exempt the garden. Commonly, endowment funds are exempt, as is real estate purchased with this fund. The fact that surplus products of a farm, beyond those used by the college, are sold does not

[49] Knox College *v.* Board of Review of Knox County, 139 N. E. (Ill.) 56.

[50] State *v.* Carleton, 191 N. W. (Minn.) 400; *in re* Syracuse University, 212 N. Y. S. 253; *see also* Emerson *v.* Trustees of Milton Academy, 185 Mass. 414; City of Gainesville *v.* Brenau College, 103 S. E. (Ga.) 164; Webb Academy *v.* City of Grand Rapids, 177 N. W. (Mich.) 290; Wheaton College *v.* Town of Norton, 122 N. E. (Mass.) 280.

[51] Appeal of St. Bridget Convent Corp., 87 Conn. 474.

[52] Trustees of Stevens Institute *v.* Bowes, 78 N. J. L. 205.

deprive the farm of exemption.[53] The rule with respect to incidental profit is well stated in Borough of Princeton *v.* Board of Taxes and Assessments: [54]

> The question being whether a school is conducted for profit . . . the test is not whether there is or may be a profit, but whether the school is conducted for the purpose of making a profit; that is, whether the charges for tuition and board are fixed with the intention of yielding a profit above the actual cost.

But private schools organized for profit are taxable.[55]

Property Rented to Others. Although there are some decisions to the contrary, property of an exempt institution leased to others for profit is subject to taxation in most cases.[56] Thus a dwelling house owned by a college and rented to a tenant is subject to taxation. Property belonging to an individual and leased to a college is taxable.[57]

Property of Educational Institutions Not Used for Educational Purposes. Such property is not exempt from taxation. Where the ground floor of a college building was occupied as a store from which income was derived, the building was exempt only to the extent of the portion used exclusively for educational purposes.[58] The decision in Girls' Friendly Society *v.* Stafford [59] announces the general rule followed under such conditions:

> . . . we think it appears that the Legislature did not . . . intend to exempt from taxation any property, either personal estate, buildings or land, of any incorporated public charitable institution, unless said property is used exclusively for educational purposes.

Other decisions fortify and support the same rule.[60]

[53] Mary Immaculate School of Eagle Park *v.* Board of Assessors, 175 N. Y. S. 701; Webb Academy *v.* City of Grand Rapids, 177 N. W. (Mich.) 290; Scott *v.* St. Johnsbury Academy, 86 Vt. 172; Dakota Wesleyan University *v.* Betts, 201 N. W. (S. D.) 524.

[54] (N. J.) 115 A. 342.

[55] Brunswick School *v.* Greenwich, 90 A. (Conn.) 801.

[56] Stahl *v.* Education Association of M. E. Church, 54 Kan. 542; State *v.* Board of Assessors, 35 La. Ann. 668; Amos *v.* Jacksonville Realty and Mortgage Co., 81 So. (Fla.) 524. *See also* Brown University *v.* Granger, 19 R. I. 704.

[57] State *v.* Macgurn, 187 Mo. 238; People *v.* Bennett Medical College, 248 Ill. 608.

[58] *In re* Syracuse University, 212 N. Y. S. 253.

[59] (R. I.) 124 A. 470.

[60] (Ill.) Knox College *v.* Board of Review, 139 N. E. 56; Commonwealth *v.* Memorial Institute, 97 S. E. (Va.) 805.

Fraternity Houses. The general rule is to subject these properties to taxation, particularly where the membership is restricted and the houses are not open to all students of the school.[61] In some instances these societies have been able to escape taxation by holding the title of the property in the name of the university, which in some states is exempt on all the property it owns. The evasion is not a legal one in the sense of coming strictly within the exemption.

Religious Societies

Cases affecting the exemption of property belonging to churches and other religious societies are numerous; and in spite of established custom and precedent, recent years have witnessed the adjudication of many such cases. This may be due (1) to the acquisition of more property by such bodies and (2) to the rising body of public opinion against so much tax exemption.

In several states the privilege of exemption is written into the constitution and is self-executing. In others, the exemption is very general and includes almost all property owned by the religious body.[62] But, generally, provision is made for relieving from taxation only that part of the property devoted exclusively to religious purposes.[63] The part of a church building rented for profits with which to pay a mortgage, and a house and lot the rentals from which help support religious exercises are not exempt.[64] In most states it is the rule to tax church property not contiguous with the lot on which the church stands, particularly if it is held as an investment or for some other source of income, and commonly if vacant and unoccupied for any purpose.[65] Although a few decisions of long standing have ruled that a leased church is exempt from taxation, this is not the general rule, and

[61] *Supra,* note 60.

[62] *In re* Dakota Wesleyan University, 202 N. W. (S. D.) 284.

[63] School of Domestic Arts and Science *v.* Carr, 322 Ill. 562; United Brethren *v.* Forsyth County Commissioners, 115 N. C. 489.

[64] First M. E. Church *v.* Chicago, 26 Ill. 482; State *v.* Union Congregational Church (Minn.), 216 N. W. 326.

[65] Green Bay & M. Canal Co. *v.* Outagamie County, 76 Wis. 587; Nevin *v.* Krollman, 38 N. J. L. 323; Presbyterian Church *v.* Montgomery County, 3 Grant Cas. 245; Enaut *v.* McGuire, 36 La. Ann. 804; Calvary Baptist Church *v.* Milliken, 147 S. W. (Ky.) 12.

a church edifice and the lot on which it stands, owned by an individual citizen, is not exempt.[66] In like manner, when a church ceases to be used as a place of worship, it ceases to be exempt from taxation.

Parsonages and Parishes

While parsonages are commonly thought of as a part of the church property, in the law of taxation they are seldom exempt.[67] Where the statutes read that property must be used exclusively for religious purposes, a parsonage or parish house cannot satisfy the requirement. This is true whether or not some religious functions are exercised in the building. In some states the parsonage is exempt from taxation if it is on the same lot with the main church edifice, while in others it is not exempt if so situated, even though the lot itself would be exempt if the parsonage were not built thereon. But there are contrary rules in a few states [68] relating to parsonage exemptions which exempt such property along with other church property. The difference lies in the strictness with which the exemption laws are written and construed.

Charitable and Benevolent Institutions

The exemption from taxation of charitable and benevolent institutions is based upon the assumption that the state would have to perform at public expense much of the work done by such institutions in their absence. In some jurisdictions the exemption laws are general and inclusive, exempting all property owned by such institutions or used largely for charitable or benevolent purposes. But the rule that has behind it the greatest weight of authority is that the property must be exclusively used for the purposes for which the institution was estab-

[66] People *v.* Anderson, 117 Ill. 50; Hebrew Free School Association *v.* City of New York, 99 N. Y. 488.

[67] Foley *v.* Congregational Church, 67 Wash. 280; Watterson *v.* Halliday, 82 N. E. (Ohio) 962; People *v.* First Congregational Church, 83 N. E. (Ill.) 536; Muldoon *v.* Board of Review, 98 N. E. (Ill.) 673; Kendrick *v.* Farquhar, 8 Ohio 187; Trustees M. E. Church *v.* Ellis, 38 Ind. 3.

[68] Notably, Iowa, Missouri, Wisconsin, South Dakota. *See* Trustees of Griswold College *v.* State, 46 Iowa 275; Bishops' Residence Co. *v.* Hudson, 90 Mo. 671, 65 Wis. 567; State *v.* Erickson, 182 N. W. (S. D.) 315.

lished or for "purely public" charity.[69] What "purely public" charity means is explained by a court in a recent decision,[70] Justice Smith delivering the opinion:

> It will be seen . . . that to give an institution the character of purely public charity two outstanding qualities are essential: First, that it must accomplish 'ends wholly benevolent' without 'profit or gain' to itself, and 'through absolute gratuity'; and, second, that in dispensing this absolute gratuity . . . it must thereby save the beneficiaries from becoming burdens upon society and the state.

Parts of buildings owned by charitable or benevolent institutions rented out for other purposes are taxable.[71] Any real property owned by such institutions which is leased for profit becomes taxable although the profits are expended for charitable purposes. But the fact that the institution may derive some profit from its property used exclusively for benevolent and charitable purposes and may apply this profit to reduce expenses does not defeat the exemption.[72] Property cannot be relieved from taxation simply because its rents and profits are applied to the support of a church or school or other charitable objects unless the property itself has been established for and is actually used for charitable purposes.[73] If property is devoted primarily to religious or charitable purposes, an incidental use for another purpose will not destroy the exemption; but an incidental use for charitable purposes will not earn exemption when the primary purpose is otherwise.[74]

PROPERTY OF Y. M. C. A.

Young Men's Christian Associations and other kindred institutions are properly classed among charitable and benevolent institutions, but a separate category is made of them in this discussion. In general, the same rules apply as in other associations

[69] *Supra,* note 62; National Navy Club *v.* City of New York, 203 N. Y. S. 114; Myers *v.* Benjamin Rose Institute, 92 Ohio St. 238; Memphis Chamber of Commerce *v.* City of Memphis, 232 S. W. (Tenn.) 73; People *v.* D. A. R., 142 N. E. 566; Webster Apartments *v.* City of New York, 193 N. Y. S. 650; Mason *v.* Zimmerman, 81 Kan. 799.

[70] City of San Antonio *v.* Santa Rosa Infirmary, 249 S. W. (Tex.) 498.

[71] M. E. Church *v.* City of Philadelphia, 109 A. (Pa.) 664.

[72] Christian Association of University of Pa. *v.* Philadelphia, 75 Pa. Super. Ct. 516.

[73] City of New Orleans *v.* St. Patrick's Hall Association, 28 La. Ann. 512.

[74] People *v.* Jessamine Withers Home, 143 N. E. (Ill.) 414.

of this kind. The real estate of a Y. M. C. A., whether the association be classed as religious or charitable, is taxable as is other real estate, when it is not used directly by the association for its own purposes. Parts of a Y. M. C. A. or a Y. W. C. A. building used for a kitchen and restaurant for serving meals to the public at a profit as well as to the occupants of the building are subject to taxation.[75] That such associations permit certain of their rooms to be used for conventions or for holding educational meetings even if receiving pay therefor does not affect the exemption of the building. In one state it was held that since a Y. M. C. A. devoted only one room out of its twenty-two to worship, such an institution was not exempt.[76] This ruling is not a common one. If it were, it would cause all such associations to be taxable.

Fraternal Orders and Social Clubs

In the constitutions or statutes of some states, fraternal orders come under the classification of charitable and benevolent bodies, and their property when solely used for charitable and benevolent purposes, and not held or leased for profit, is exempt from taxation.[77] When such is the grounds on which exemption is claimed, the mere casual use of a portion of the property of such orders for some purpose other than the main one to which the institution is dedicated, will not affect the exemption. The numerous decisions from the courts of last resort among the states disclose the fact that the majority of fraternal orders are unable to earn exemption under the "charitable and benevolent" clause of the statutes for several reasons, among them: (1) because the social functions of the order are tantamount to any benevolent and charitable work undertaken; (2) a large portion of the property is often rented out for stores and other mercantile purposes; (3) the institution's facilities are often rented to other kindred organizations for lodge purposes at a stipulated rental; and (4) the benefits extended from dues and

[75] Y. M. C. A. *v.* City of New York, 216 N. Y. S. 248; City of Auburn *v.* Y. M. C. A. of Auburn, 86 Me. 244.

[76] Y. M. C. A. *v.* New York City, 113 N. Y. 187.

[77] *In re* Masonic Temple Society, 111 S. E. (W. Va.) 637; Syracuse Masonic Temple *v.* Ostrander, 173 N. Y. S. 356.

other sources of income accrue particularly to the members of the order in the form of sick and death benefits, hospital care, and the like, and not to the public in general.

Hence it has been recently held[78] that a building belonging to a fraternal order, organized for fraternal and benevolent purposes, and to manage and conduct a social club, the lower floor of which was used for a kitchen and social and recreation rooms, is not exempt from taxation. The same decision recites that the payment of sick and death benefits to members regardless of their need also militates against the privilege of exemption. Another decision[79] renders the same class of property subject to taxation on the additional grounds of leasing the lodge's facilities to other lodges for their ritualistic work, with the injunction that such uses of the property do not meet the requirement of carrying out the religious, charitable, and educational purposes of the order's organization. In Appeal of Scottish Rite Building Co.,[80] the court employed the following language in regard to such exemptions:

> The question of fact, therefore, is whether or not the building in question was, in a practical sense, used for charitable purposes, and it cannot be held to have been so used unless charity was actually dispensed there, or unless it provided necessary quarters for an organization whose prime purposes and functions were actively charitable.

There is authority for saying that where part of a building belonging to a fraternal order is rented out for profit, and the remaining devoted to purposes of the association, only the rented part is taxable.[81] Yet most of the authority points to the rule that the whole property is subject to taxation when any considerable part is devoted to other purposes.[82]

The property of social clubs which incidentally dispense charity is not entitled to exemption under any statutes, although some clubs have attempted to acquire exemption under the "charitable" cloak of the statute.[83]

[78] People *ex rel* Loyal Order of Moose *v.* Clark, 210 N. Y. S. 353.

[79] I. O. O. F. *v.* Burke, 126 N. Y. S. 944.

[80] (Nebr.) 182 N. W. 574.

[81] Odd Fellows Building Association *v.* Naylor, 177 P. 214.

[82] Masonic Hall Association *v.* White, 214 N. Y. S. 390; Wilson *v.* Licking Aerie, 135 N. E. (Ohio) 545; W. O. W. *v.* City of San Angelo, 231 S. W. (Tex.) 1106; I. O. O. F. *v.* City of Lexington, 194 S. W. (Ky.) 92.

[83] New Standard Club *v.* McRaven, 71 So. (Miss.) 289.

Hospitals, Asylums, Almshouses

The one general basis upon which hospitals can claim and acquire the exemption privilege is the manner in which the institution is carried on. If conducted as a business with the understanding that profits are to be divided among certain individuals, they are not exempt. The fact that they dispense charity to a limited number of people is immaterial.[84] "The theory upon which charitable hospitals are exempt from taxation is that their chief object and accomplishment is to care for those who would otherwise become charges upon the state or society, so that the care of patients who are able to and who do pay therefor is not charity." But hospitals carried on by means of gifts and donations and open to all without charge, even though some can and do pay for such service, are exempt.[85] A recent Kansas decision[86] enunciates the principle upon which exemption is clearly earned:

> When an institution is incorporated for benevolent purposes without capital stock and no dividends are declared or paid, and conducts a hospital, and all earnings of the hospital from pay patients, all gifts, devises, bequests, or income from whatever source, are used in the maintenance, extension, and improvement of the hospital, and which admits patients without regard to race, creed, or wealth, it is uniformly held that such hospital is conducted exclusively for charitable purposes.

Property of a hospital corporation not used exclusively for the purposes of the organization is not exempt. Nurses' homes situated on a different lot than was the hospital were held taxable in a Mississippi decision.[87] But a farm permanently used by a hospital for an open-air sanitarium and incidently for profit to reduce running expenses, though separated from the main hospital, was declared not subject to taxation in Pennsylvania.[88] These two decisions are typical of the divergence of opinion on what constitutes an exclusive use.

Poor farms and all land used for necessary pasturage, for

[84] City of San Antonio *v.* Santa Rosa Infirmary, 249 S. W. (Tex.) 498; City of Knoxville *v.* Ft. Sanders Hospital, 257 S. W. (Tenn.) 408.

[85] Proctor Hospital *v.* Board of Review, 233 Ill. 583.

[86] Nuns of Third Order of St. Dominic *v.* Younkin, 118 Kan. 554.

[87] Johnson *v.* Mississippi Baptist Hospital, 106 So. (Miss.) 1.

[88] Pa. Hospital *v.* Delaware County, 169 Pa. 305.

crops, and for keeping stock, are commonly exempt in all states.[89] Asylums are by their very nature exempt from taxation. It has even been held that a hospital for animals operated by a society for the prevention of cruelty to animals is exempt as a benevolent and charitable institution.[90]

Libraries and Museums

Library property is usually property of the state or municipality and therefore not taxable on that account. It is commonly exempt whether public property or not, and the fact that it charges a fee for book rentals does not defeat the exemption. But where a building is only partly used for library purposes, the remaining part, if used for other purposes, is taxable.[91]

Museums and like property, unless conducted for a profit, are exempt from taxation.

Cemeteries and Burial Grounds

"The obvious impropriety of selling the graves of the dead to pay the expenses of carrying on the government of the living" is said to be one reason for not taxing cemeteries and burial grounds. Such property, when used exclusively for cemetery purposes, is exempt from taxation in almost every state. With respect to that part of a cemetery not devoted to burial purposes, the statutes and decisions are not in agreement. Nor are they with respect to the capital stock of associations owning such property. In several instances [92] unoccupied land of the association is subject to taxation. Particularly is this true where there is doubt that the land ever will be used for burial purposes. Other rulings [93] are to the effect that land within the boundaries of the cemetery although not yet occupied by graves is not taxable. Some states exempt the capital stock, others do not.[94]

[89] Town of Hamden *v.* City of New Haven, 101 (Conn.) 11.

[90] Mass. Society, etc., *v.* City of Boston, 142 Mass. 24.

[91] Mercantile Library Co. *v.* Philadelphia, 14 Pa. C. Ct. R. 204. *Same,* 161 Pa. 155.

[92] Fairview Development Co. *v.* Fay, 90 N. J. L. 427; Mt. Pleasant Cemetery Co. *v.* City of Newark, 98, A. (N. J.) 448; People *v.* Graceland Cemetery Co., 86 Ill. 336; Rosehill Cemetery Co. *v.* Kern, 147 Ill. 483.

[93] City of Hoboken *v.* Inhabitants of North Bergen Tp., 3 N. J. L. 146.

[94] Metairie Cemetery Association *v.* Board of Assessors, 37 La. Ann. 32; Oak Ridge Cemetery Corp. *v.* Tax Commission, 132 N. E. (Ill.) 553.

The fact that a cemetery association is in receipt of revenue from the sale of lots or from the rental of the unused portion of the grounds, although realizing a profit for the association does not usually invalidate the exemption in most jurisdictions.[95] But other property which a cemetery association might own and from which it derives profit to assist in maintaining the cemetery, is not exempt from taxation on that account. Until the statutes are amended in many states it will be impossible to tax cemetery corporations organized for profit with the expectation of paying dividends to stockholders. However, to organize a business similar to a cemetery association and to expect it to be exempt under cover of such similarity, is more than some states will tolerate. In Mausoleum Builders of New Jersey *v.* State Board of Taxes and Assessments,[96] builders of mausoleums claimed exemption on the grounds of being part of a cemetery association. The court bluntly said:

> Neither the language of the tax enactment nor its history suggests that in passing it the legislature intended to confer immunity from taxation upon business corporations that should see fit to devote a part of their capital to the erection of mausoleums for purely commercial reasons . . . nor any purpose to authorize the corporations to whom such immunity is granted to transfer the exemption to corporations of the character just described.

Transfer, Assignability, and Revocation of the Exemption

An exemption from taxation for any purpose is a personal privilege conferred on an individual or a corporation and does not carry with it the right[97] of transfer. This right can be given only by legislative action. Where property owned by an organization, which under the law is exempt, is sold to one not exempt, the property becomes taxable unless the purchaser likewise is an exempt individual or corporation. Where one church purchases the property of another, exemption does not need to be

[95] Hope Cemetery Association *v.* Rose, 191 N. Y. S. 623; City of Paducah *v.* Commonwealth, 124 S. W. (Ky.) 286; State *v.* Crystal Lake Cemetery Association, 193 N. W. (Minn.) 170.

[96] 100 A. 236, affirming judgment 88 N. J. L. 592.

[97] State *v.* Great Northern Ry. Co., 116 Minn. 303, judgment affirmed 216 U. S. 206; Commonwealth *v.* Owensboro & N. R. Co., 81 Ky. 572.

transferred. But property owned by a church congregation and sold to a purchaser for use other than for religious purposes immediately loses immunity from taxation. This is true after title has passed although the congregation still continues to use the church, paying some compensation therefor.[98]

The question as to whether the property is taxable for the year when the exemption ceases is answered by determining the ownership on the tax date or the assessment date in the particular jurisdiction. If the property, formerly exempt, is sold and transferred before the tax date, it is assessable for taxation for the ensuing year; if it is sold and the title passes after the tax date, the property remains exempt until the next date at which taxes are assessed. The same rule applies under conditions where taxable property is purchased or transferred to owners or purposes creating an immunity from taxation.[99]

Taxes already due are in no way relieved by the passage of exemption enactments nor by the property's coming under exemption privileges.

It has been stated that exemption is either constitutional, statutory, charter, or contractual. Either creation is by the sovereign power and therefore revocable by the same authority unless such repeal would impair the obligation of a contract, forbidden by the United States Constitution.[100] Since exemption continues only so long as the property is devoted to the purposes for which specified, the power of revocation is employed to restore to a taxable status any property failing to continue under the provisions of the immunity.

Summary

1. One fifth of the nation's taxable wealth is exempt from taxation.

2. School officials should know what property is exempt and under what conditions to assure themselves that all of the

[98] Havens *v.* Alameda County, 157 P. (Cal.) 821; Town of New Haven *v.* Sheffield, 30 Conn. 160; Commonwealth *v.* First Presbyterian Church, 183 S. W. (Ky.) 943.

[99] Berger *v.* University of New Mexico, 217 P. (N. M.) 245; New York *v.* Tax, etc., Commissioners, 104 U. S. 466.

[100] State *v.* Kelly, 119 S. E. (N. C.) 755; Berger *v.* University of New Mexico, 217 P. (N. M.) 245.

school's property entitled to exemption is immune from taxation and that no property is hiding under the cloak of exemption unless clearly exempt by statute.

3. The source of exemption lies in the state.

4. Property is generally exempt for the following reasons:
   a. Owned by an individual or institution which is exempt.
   b. Used for purposes entitling it to exemption under the statutes.
   c. Both ownership and use.

5. Statutes granting exemption are strictly construed, but there is a tendency to a more liberal construction when religious, charitable, benevolent, and educational institutions are concerned.

6. State and federal agencies and instrumentalities cannot be taxed.

7. Public school property is exempt when title is in the board of education. Property leased from an individual for school purposes is not exempt. And school property leased to individuals for other than educational purposes is taxable.

8. Colleges and similar educational institutions are exempt as to their property used exclusively for educational purposes. Contiguous property is exempt when used for reasonably necessary purposes. Property leased to others for profit is taxable, as is property leased from an individual for educational purposes.

9. Religious societies are exempt as to property used strictly for the purposes for which the institution was established. But property rented for profit is taxable. Parsonages are not commonly exempt, but the contrary is true in some states.

10. Charitable and benevolent institutions are exempt as to property used exclusively for "purely public" charity under most jurisdictions. Some statutes are more liberal. Parts of buildings of such institutions not devoted to the purposes of the organization are taxable. The mere application of incidental profits to charity does not warrant the exemption of such institutions.

11. Fraternity orders and social clubs have difficulty in meriting the exemption privilege because
   a. Social functions are paramount to charitable work;
   b. Much of their property is devoted to other purposes;

c. They rent parts of their rooms to other organizations; and

d. Their sick and death benefits accrue to only their own members.

In some states they are exempt as to all property belonging to the order; but the general rule exempts only such property devoted to public charity.

12. Hospitals are exempt when not organized and conducted for business purposes and dispense charity gratuitously. Asylums are exempt.

13. Libraries and museums are not taxable as to property used therefor.

14. Cemeteries are commonly exempt from taxation. In some jurisdictions, property not used or likely to be used soon for burial purposes is taxable, while in others it is exempt. Mausoleums, when erected by a business corporation, are not exempt.

15. The exemption privilege is not transferable nor assignable.

CHAPTER V

PRINCIPLES PERTAINING TO THE LEVY AND ASSESSMENT OF SCHOOL DISTRICT TAXES

Nature of Levy and Assessment

Prerequisite to any collection of a valid tax upon the property of a school district are two important and indispensable acts. The first of these is the levy of the tax; the second, the assessment of the property upon which the levy is imposed. Although they are sometimes erroneously spoken of as one and the same act, the terms are separate and distinct in meaning and occupy a distinct and specific place in the law of taxation. Many decisions in both the state supreme courts and in the United States courts have set forth the distinction between the two terms or acts.

The term "levy" refers to the ascertainment of a sum to be imposed upon the taxpayers and the legal imposition of that sum as an obligation on the collective body of taxpayers. It also declares the subjects and the rate of taxation.[1] A tax levy is a purely legislative function, the formal vote or action of the body authorized to make the levy and not the mere ministerial act of ascertaining the rate per cent. Fixing the rate is not a complete levy.[2] The mere act of a board of education ordering that a levy be made for the future on previous assessment is not an actual levy.

The original source of the power to levy is, of course, the constitution of the state legislature. "The rule is one which applies to federal taxation and to taxation for state purposes or for municipal purposes or for local assessments."[3] Since we have

[1] Hilliard, *Taxation*, p. 290; Sussex County *v.* Jarratt, 106 S. E. (Va.) 384; Morton *v.* Comptroller General, 4 S. C. 430; State *v.* Council of Minneapolis, 161 Minn. 103.

[2] Morrison *v.* Moir Hotel Co., 204 Ill. App. 433; Purington *v.* Broughton (Tex.), 158 S. W. 227; *supra*, note 1; *post*, note 4.

[3] Cooley, "Taxation," Vol. 3, Chap. 17.

shown that the power to tax may be and is delegated to the local political subdivisions, it is not necessary to include at this point a discussion relative to the delegation of the power to levy the tax, levy being one of the parts of the whole proceeding in taxation.[4] This brings us to the fact that the levy of a local tax by a local authority involves two distinct acts of legislation: (1) that by the state giving the power to tax, and (2) that by the local legislative or quasi-legislative authority, laying the tax under the power so given.[5]

It is well settled that the power to levy a tax can be delegated only to duly authorized officers or bodies acting in a legislative capacity and not to mere ministerial officers. If the levy is made by unauthorized officers it cannot be subsequently ratified by the authorized body. So it was held [6] that a board of trustees of a civil town having no authority to levy a tax for a special school fund, such unauthorized levy could not be legalized by ratification by the board of trustees of the school town. Justice Miller, delivering the opinion of the court, said, among other things:

> In our opinion, the levy made by the town trustees, being wholly without their jurisdiction, was void, and the subsequent adoption and ratification by the trustees of the school town of this unauthorized levy did not impart to it vitality and effectiveness. . . . We know of no principle of law that would authorize such delegation of power, and we cannot, therefore, see how there could be an adoption or ratification by one board of the acts of the other.

In spite of the fact that the term "levy" is often held to include not only the ascertainment of the amount necessary to be raised, but also the performance of all such acts as would authorize the tax collector to proceed to collect the tax, the "assessment" is equally important in all taxation procedure. Every assessment must rest upon a proper levy, and if there is no levy there can be no assessment.[7] But, if there is no assessment upon the levy, there can be no collection of the tax.

The term "assessment" means the process by which persons subject to taxation are listed, their property described, and its

[4] School Dist. No. 127 *v.* School Dist. No. 45 of Reno County, 80 Kan. 641.

[5] *Supra,* note 3; Board of Education of Ogden *v.* Brown, 12 Utah 251.

[6] Shepardson *v.* Gillette, 133 Ind. 125; *see also* 108 N. W. (Wis.) 557.

[7] Sussex County *v.* Jarratt, 106 S. E. (Va.) 384; McGinnis *v.* Nelson County, 146 Va. 170.

cash value ascertained and stated.[8] Sometimes two meanings are given to the term; the one refers to the listing and valuing of the property, and the other also includes the calculation of the rate and amount of taxes upon the property so described and valued.[9] Assessment is a quasi-judicial function.[10] If it is impossible to conform to the prescribed law in making the assessment, then no tax can be levied, for it is uniformly required that a valid assessment is essential to a valid tax.[11]

Conditions Precedent to the Levy and Assessment

If there are prerequisites essential to the levy and assessment of the tax written into the tax laws, they must be observed or the tax will not be valid. If no such preliminaries are by law required, the validity of the tax does not depend upon them.[12] Such prerequisites may include:

1. The filing of a petition for the levy.[13]
2. An order by some court or judge directing the levy to be made.[14]
3. The legal designation of a building site or similar act.[15]
4. Submission of the question to popular vote.[16]
5. Making by other officers of an estimate of expenses required.[17]

It is also usually required that every essential proceeding in the course of a levy and assessment of taxes must appear on some written record of the bodies authorized to act upon them. In other words, the parol levy of taxes is impossible. If the records have been lost, evidence must show that they at one time existed or a sale of property for failure to pay taxes will be void.[18]

[8] Butte Electric Ry. Co. *v.* McIntyre, 227 P. (Mont.) 61; People *v.* Priest, 169 N. Y. 432.

[9] Flanigan *v.* Police Judge of Jackson Parish, 145 La. 613.

[10] Hilliard, *Taxation,* p. 29; Sussex Co. *v.* Jarratt, 106 S. E. (Va.) 384; Morton *v.* Comptroller General, 4 S. C. 430.

[11] State *v.* Gehner, 286 S. W. (Mo.) 117; State *v.* Hamilton, 293 S. W. (Mo.) 378; State *v.* Williams, 216 S. W. (Mo.) 536; Joliet Stove Works *v.* Kilp, 230 Ill. 550.

[12] School Dist. of Omaha *v.* City of Omaha, 39 Neb. 745; Hewes *v.* Reis, 40 Cal. 255.

[13] Williams *v.* Hall, 65 Ind. 129.

[14] Couper *v.* Rowe, 42 Ga. 229.

[15] Gustin *v.* School Dist., 10 Gray (Mass.) 85.

[16] Murphy *v.* Harbison, 29 Ark. 340.

[17] Kirchner *v.* Wapsinonoc School Township, 141 Iowa 43.

[18] Fagan *v.* Rosier, 68 Ill. 84; Moore *v.* Cooke, 40 Iowa 290; Moser v. White, 29 Mich. 59.

If certain conditions must be fulfilled, the statutes are called mandatory; if the law does not require but prescribe that they may be fulfilled, the statutes are directory. The courts' decisions are not in any agreement as to whether certain specific acts are to be classed as mandatory or directory, as can be seen from the following quotation: [19]

> In considering the various statutes regulating the assessment of taxes . . . it is not always easy to distinguish which are conditions precedent to the legality and validity of the tax, and which are directory merely. . . . One rule is very plain and well settled—that all those measures which are intended for the security of the citizen, for ensuring an equality of taxation, and to enable every one to know with reasonable certainty for what polls and for what real and personal estate he is taxed . . . are conditions precedent; and if they are not observed, he is not legally taxed. . . .

It is therefore generally agreed that those legislative directions that have for their object the protection of the taxpayer against spoliation are mandatory; but if the regulations are intended to promote method and system and uniformity, they are directory. So ministerial and clerical duties, the observance or nonobservance of which do not affect the taxpayer injuriously, are classed as directory.[20] Justice Stone in the above-cited case continues the argument:

> There is much contrariety of opinion in the adjudged cases, on the question when statutory provisions for assessing and collecting taxes are mandatory, and when they are simply directory. No amount of learning or of logic can reconcile the various rulings. In some of the states great strictness in the observance of statutory regulations is required; while in others liberal intendments are indulged in favor of the correct performance of duties the law casts on the officials. . . .

It is necessary that the assessment be made by a duly elected and qualified assessor chosen by the qualified voters of the school district.[21] Where an assessment is made by an assessor not so elected and qualified, it is void and tax collection can be enjoined. Likewise, it is imperative that the board levying the tax

[19] Torrey *v.* Milbury, 21 Pick. 64.

[20] State *v.* Jackson County, 65 Ala. 142, rehearing P. 166.

[21] Odem *v.* Sinton Independent School Dist., 234 S. W. (Tex.) 1090; People *v.* Stockton & C. R. Co., 49 Cal. 414.

be surrounded by certain definite formalities or injustice may often result. The board must act by majority and usually in a regular meeting (although levies have been pronounced valid if made in other than regular meetings) at a time and a place specified by law. So in a case where the record of proceedings of a board did not show how many members were present, how many voted on the motion, and how they voted individually or as a body, it was held that the proceedings did not comply with the law, and therefore caused a void levy.[22]

The vote of the people at the annual school meeting alone is not sufficient to create a valid levy. They may give the authority, by their vote, to levy the tax, but the board of education alone can execute the power of declaring the tax levied. This act may be a mere formality of filling out forms, attaching signatures, and certifying the levy to the proper authorities, but it is essential to the actual levy of a tax.

If it is required by law that the vote of a board of education authorizing a tax levy be taken by yeas and nays, a disregard of this injunction will nullify the levy; and an amendatory resolution passed after a change in the board's membership has taken place will not make the levy valid. If the statutes do not require the yeas and nays, it is only necessary to show on the records that there was a quorum present, and that a majority voted for the levy.[23] In some states the district authorities are limited to levying a tax for educational and building purposes only. Under such conditions it is not legal to levy taxes for any purpose which cannot be classified under at least one of those two divisions. It has even been held that to levy a tax for transportation of pupils in a consolidated district was illegal since it is not authorized by legislative enactment. But, generally, in the absence of the express legislative authority to levy taxes for such a purpose, the courts have ruled that since it is necessary to transport the children before they can be subjected to the school's educative influence, the purpose is included as an educational one. It has also

[22] Geffert *v.* Yorktown Indep. School Dist., 290 S. W. (Tex.) 1083; People *v.* New York Cent. Ry. Co., 145 N. E. (Ill.) 593; Gilbert *v.* Huston, Litt. Sel. Cas. (Ky.) 223; Gamble *v.* Witty, 55 Miss. 26; People *v.* Chicago & E. I. Ry Co., 145 N. E. (Ill.) 670.

[23] Pontiac *v.* Axford, 49 Mich. 69.

become settled that the express authority to levy a tax for building purposes includes the implied authority to levy for the purchase of land upon which to erect the building. In some jurisdictions, it is necessary that the building be decided upon by a vote of the people before a tax may be levied for its erection. In such a case, it is illegal to levy a tax to create a fund for use in the future as a building fund when the building has not been decided upon.[24]

The Making, the Validity, and the Requisites of Levy and Assessment

In the previous discussion of conditions precedent to the valid levy and assessment of taxes, it was noted that certain prerequisites are often essential to such levy and assessment. Those conditions are precedent to the act. The present discussion has as its object the presentation of facts dealing with the making of the levy, the doing of certain acts which may invalidate the levy, the omission of acts which may invalidate it, and other requisites either directory or mandatory. There are many clauses in the tax statutes either directory or mandatory accordingly as the intent of the lawmakers is interpreted by the courts. As has been mentioned before,[25] there is little agreement among the adjudged cases on many of the points to be herein discussed. Much depends upon the wording of the statute and the construction placed upon it by the courts in each jurisdiction. There are a few rules of quite general acceptance. These will be singled out for emphasis.

In the first place, the validity of any tax is based upon a valid levy upon which is dependent a valid assessment.[26] Along with these must appear a written record of the different proceedings as before discussed. Second, the essential question to determine is whether constitutional and statutory provisions as to uniformity and equality have been observed. Third, legislative acts to be performed by the school trustees are generally mandatory, but the courts will sustain a levy though technically defective, when-

[24] St. Louis, A. & F. H. Ry. Co. *v.* State, 224 Ill. 155; People *v.* Bell, 309 Ill. 433.

[25] *See* page 76.

[26] Bennett *v.* Finkbine Lumber Co., 199 Iowa 1085.

ever there is sufficient proof to make the intent of the levying body conformable with the statutes.[27] Fourth, ministerial acts are directory and usually do not affect the validity of the levy.

Some ministerial and technical acts will be presented for illustration. A mistake by the county clerk in extending the tax upon the rolls at a lower rate than the district levied does not invalidate the levy so extended although the district cannot collect the difference in revenue between their levy and the one extended by the county clerk. They are entitled to what revenue the extended levy produced.[28] The ousting of the board of education will operate to invalidate an attempted tax levy by the district which has not even a de facto board.[29] Taxpayers who for a number of years have not objected to their inclusion in an extended district, and who have paid their proportion of the taxes, cannot thereafter question the validity of the taxes they have paid and are soon to pay, upon the grounds of an illegal extension of the district.[30] Some statutes declare that the purposes for which a tax is to be levied must be designated. Under such statute it is held that "for incidentals" is not sufficiently clear and invalidates the levy. Under other laws, the reverse is true.[31] If levies for educational and building purposes are required by law to be kept separate, to include them in one levy is a fatal error.[32]

The Time of Levy

In all states there are laws governing the time when estimates are to be submitted, when levies are to be voted by the authorized body, when such levies are to be certified to the proper ministerial officers for extension on the tax roll, and when other acts are to be performed. The question arises, how strictly must such regulations be followed? If the required act is not done at the time specified, is the levy void on that account?

Here again, the statutes and decisions are not in harmony. But the weight of authority is on the side of declaring the ele-

[27] Smith *v.* Hurlburt, 108 Or. 690.

[28] School Dist. No. 127 *v.* School Dist. No. 45 of Reno County, 80 Kan. 641.

[29] People *v.* New York Cent. Ry. Co., 119 N. E. (Ill.) 299.

[30] Carr *v.* Little, 123 S. E. (N. C.) 625.

[31] State *v.* Walfrom, 25 Wis. 468; State *v.* Cole, 18 A. (N. J.) 52; West School Dist. of Canton *v.* Merrils, 12 Conn. 437.

[32] State *v.* Wabash, St. L. & P. Ry. Co., 90 Mo. 166.

ment of time to be merely directory and that a tax is not void if levied after the prescribed time.[33] A Wyoming decision [34] illustrates the more liberal interpretation of the courts by stating that, although the levy is required by statute to be made on the first Monday of September, if made and the tax roll delivered so as to give the taxpayer reasonable opportunity to pay his taxes before they become delinquent, he has no grounds for complaint. Thus it is seen that the failure to certify a school tax by the school directors by the day named in the statutes does not invalidate the tax, but is a mere irregularity. It is well settled that events happening after the levy has been properly made have no effect on the validity of the levy. But it is not difficult to find decisions contrary to the ones just mentioned.[35]

Taxes Levied in Excess of the Legal Limit

It has been previously stated that the power of the state to levy taxes is unlimited except as provided by the constitution. Legislatures have, in general, been vested with plenary powers in matters of taxation. Clothed with such power, they have found it necessary to prescribe limits beyond which the taxing subdivisions of the state cannot go. Usually the limit is expressed as a certain mill rate on a certain valuation of property; or, it may be a definite rate of a prescribed percentage of the aggregate value of taxable property.

The limit of indebtedness has nothing to do with the amount of taxes a district can levy unless such levy is to increase the indebtedness beyond the statutory limit. In other words, a district already indebted to the legal limit may still vote taxes for current expenses. Hence it is obvious that when we speak of a tax levy beyond the legal limit, we must bear in mind that it may have two implications, one referring to the creating of a bonded indebtedness, the other to the prescribed limit for current expenditures.

The question for consideration here is not, Can districts go

[33] Buck *v.* People, 78 Ill. 560; Moore *v.* Fessenbeck, 88 Ill. 422; Thatcher *v.* People, 79 Ill. 597; Williams *v.* Lunenberg School Dist. No. 1, 21 Pick. (Mass.) 75.

[34] Baker *v.* Paxton, 215 P. (Wyo.) 257.

[35] Gamble *v.* Witty, 55 Miss. 26; People *v.* Wabash Ry. Co., 129 N. E. (Ill.) 826; People *v.* Chicago, M. & St. P. Ry. Co., 142 N. E. (Ill.) 167.

beyond the legal limit in matters of taxation? but, What is the outcome if they do exceed the legal limit? Laws would be of no effect if not enforceable. But it often occurs that districts levy a tax beyond the limit prescribed by statute without realizing their error until after the levy has been imposed. Is the levy, therefore, void? Is it totally void, or only void in the amount exceeding the legal limit? Obviously, the principle, "illegal in part, illegal as a whole," would work numerous hardships on school districts inadvertently exceeding the legal tax limit. Fortunately, a long series of decisions casts its whole weight on one side. Taxes levied in excess of the statutory limit are void only as to the excess above the statutory limit,[36] unless the illegality so permeates the whole tax that the legal cannot be separated from the illegal tax.

Where a common school district and a high school district are coterminous, but under different boards, the question of the tax limit may involve both districts. Each may be surrounded by a statutory limitation on its own account, or the statute may cover a particular territory and refer to both districts together, or both conditions may prevail.[37]

It should be remembered that the limitation placed upon the amount of taxes that can be levied in any one year does not limit the amount that can be expended for a certain purpose over a period of years.[38] In determining whether the limit of indebtedness in a district has been reached, only its own debts are to be considered and not those of the municipality with which it may be coexistent, unless specifically provided otherwise by statute, as in the case of some fiscally dependent cities. The district is entitled to deduct all available assets on hand in computing the limit.[39]

A slightly different angle presents itself when the tax is levied

[36] Kirchener *v.* Wapsinonoc School Township, 118 N. W. (Ia.) 51; People *v.* Peoria, etc., R. Co., 216 Ill. 22; Colton *v.* Beardsley, 38 Barb. 29; Trustees of White School Dist. No. 15 *v.* Cummins, 33 Ky. Law. Rep. 739; People *v.* Cairo V. & C. Ry. Co., 94 N. E. (Ill.) 11; Elyton Land Co. *v.* Birmingham, 89 Ala. 477; Young *v.* Henderson, 76 N. C. 420; State *v.* School Dist. No. 3 of Jackson County, 121 Kan. 573; Flanders *v.* Board of Trustees of Little Rock Graded School, 170 Ky. 627; Schaff *v.* Rea, 103 Okla. 62.

[37] Welch *v.* Getzen, 85 S. C. 156.

[38] Robbins *v.* Anoka County School Dist. No. 1, 10 Minn. 340.

[39] Wilson *v.* Huron Board of Education, 12 S. D. 535.

to pay an already unconstitutional debt. In such cases it is held that the whole tax is void. Warrants issued by a district beyond the legal limit of indebtedness cannot be paid out of a legal tax. The tax itself becomes illegal.[40]

In the absence of any constitutional or statutory limitation prohibiting school districts from levying taxes, the general rule followed is that the district may incur indebtedness and levy taxes for any legitimate and necessary purpose within reason.

Back Assessment and Omitted Taxes

To collect all the taxes on all the taxable property during any one year in every political subdivision of the state is beyond the vainest dreams of the tax officers. Property escapes taxation through both intent and inadvertence. The amount of revenue lost because of omitted taxes must be large. Figures are not obtainable to indicate how great the loss is annually.

Before proceeding with the legal phase of this topic, the distinction between omitted taxes and delinquent taxes must be made. Delinquent taxes are taxes accrued and due but unpaid. They have been levied and assessed, but collection of them has failed. Omitted taxes, on the other hand, result from failure to list and assess the property on which taxes are payable. This failure to assess may result from the negligence of the officials responsible therefor; or it may be the direct act of the taxpayer in failing to list or return his property for taxation. For the reason that omitted taxes are due to failure to assess, it is necessary to "back assess" such property before the collector has a legitimate warrant for collection of taxes on the property.

Back assessment may also be made upon property which has been previously greatly undervalued. The authority for a reassessment of property lies in the legislature. Unless there is expressed statutory power to reassess, the school district cannot call upon the responsible officers for an assessment of property omitted from the tax rolls or a back assessment of undervalued property. While in some states there are constitutional restraints on the passage of retroactive legislation, the courts generally hold that statutory regulations for back assessment are not repugnant

[40] People *v.* Toledo, P. & W. Ry. Co., 229 Ill. 327.

to the constitutional inhibition. In rendering the opinion of the court in a case [41] reaching the United States Supreme Court from Ohio, Justice Wood takes occasion to refute the argument that Ohio's prohibition against retroactive legislation should be applicable to tax legislation. He says in part:

> In substance the contention is that a taxpayer, who has been evading the payment of the taxes due from him by making false returns, can shield himself behind the annual settlement . . . in which his returns were said to be true, and that the legislature can pass no act by which the falsity of the returns can for a limited number of years, be exposed, and the payment of the taxes enforced. . . . Such a proposition cannot be sustained.

In another decision,[42] the placing of omitted property on the assessment books is clearly upheld in the following language:

> If assessable property has been omitted from the assessment books or has escaped assessment when it ought to have been assessed, the fact that it has not been discovered and valued and placed upon the assessment books until after the levy has been made, cannot release its owner from paying taxes on account thereof, and cannot defeat the right of the state or the municipality to demand and collect those taxes.

The mere fact that school expenditures have been paid for the years in which the taxes were omitted or that the particular school purpose for which they were levied no longer exists, or even that the omitted taxes may create a surplus in the school fund—none of these facts presents any legal grounds why such property should continue to escape its share of the support of public schools. When collected, such taxes may be appropriated as any other surplus, and thereby lessen the burden of taxation on those who for certain years have paid more than their share for school support.[43]

The question at once arises, at what valuation shall omitted property be back assessed? The question can be answered only in the light of legislative enactments in the various states them-

[41] Sturgis *v.* Carter, 114 U. S. 511.

[42] Hopkins *v.* Van Wyck, 80 Md. 7; *see also* Farmers M. Bank *v.* Vandalia, 57 Ill. App. 681; Aggers *v.* People, 20 Colo. 348; Anderson *v.* Ritterbusch, 98 P. (Okla.) 1002; Olmstead *v.* Barber, 31 Minn. 256; Fairfield *v.* People, 94 Ill. 244; Byro *v.* Detroit, 50 Mich. 56.

[43] Anderson *v.* Ritterbusch, 98 P. (Okla.) 1002; Village of Hyde Park *v.* Ingalls, 87 Ill. 11.

selves. The statutes must be strictly followed. If they require that the assessment be at a valuation as of the year the property was omitted, or that the valuation be as of the current year, there is no alternative. The general rule is that the valuation is left to the discretion of the assessor.[44]

The right of school officials to demand a back assessment of omitted property is therefore unquestioned. Unless prohibited by the statutes of limitations, they may demand taxes that have been lost to the district on omitted property for any number of years. Their right to do so is well settled by a long and unbroken line of decisions and by text writers on assessment. To do less than their duty in demanding such taxes is to be guilty of laying a heavier burden upon other taxpayers.

Excessive and Fraudulent Levy

It is possible to keep within the legal limits and yet levy a tax that is excessive or even fraudulent. In the absence of express legislation, it has become a matter of public policy not to interfere with the discretion of the board of education as to the raising and expending of funds unless there is manifest abuse of the power reposed in such a board. But taxpayers should have some safeguard whereby to protect their property from an excessive burden and public funds from spoliation. For example, the arbitrary assessment of property for school purposes at three times the valuation for state and county purposes, without reference to the fair market value, imposes a burden upon the taxpayer not contemplated by the constitution or the legislature in granting the power to levy and assess to school district officers.[45] So it is held that a taxpayer may maintain an action to prevent the district board from involving the district in an unwarrantable expenditure.[46] But there is always the presumption that the tax is just and that the board has discharged its duties in a proper and faithful manner. Therefore, the burden of proof that such board acted improperly or fraudulently is squarely upon the one claiming such misconduct.[47] It is not possible in

[44] Burroughs on "Assessment," p. 197; *see also* People *v.* Goff, 52 N. Y. 434.
[45] Power *v.* Andrews, 253 S. W. (Texas) 870.
[46] Lindeman *v.* Corson, 141 N. W. (Neb.) 153.
[47] People *v.* Bates, 107 N. E. (Ill.) 123.

most jurisdictions for a city council to refuse to levy the tax sufficient to raise the required revenue, unless the council can show that the board acted in bad faith or embraced unlawful items in their demand.[48] Common reason in addition to the weight of authority decrees that a board of education cannot estimate with exactitude the amount required for such things as repairs, replacements, and improvements and an amount raised in excess of such needs does not render the act fraudulent in any sense of the word.[49]

Acts Antecedent and Subsequent to Levy and Assessment

There remain several questions concerning levy and assessment which have not been answered. The first is, Is property taxable in the absence of a levy? The answer is, no. Levy and assessment are two essentials of the procedure in taxation.[50]

Can a school district make two levies in one year? It depends upon the circumstances. If a levy is tardy for the current year, it and the levy for the following year may be levied the same year. Again, in the case a levy has been declared void it becomes the duty of the board in most jurisdictions to make a new levy. However, since the time for presenting the levy is generally fixed in most states, it becomes impossible to make more than one levy unless, as before stated, the previous one has been set aside.[51]

Does a mistake of a ministerial officer in extending the tax rate on the rolls invalidate the levy? It does not, but the funds raised by the wrong levy are all the district is entitled to. This applies, of course, after the rate has been spread and taxes actually become due. If the act can be intercepted before this takes place, the proper court procedure will remedy the levy.[52]

Do taxes levied constitute a fund against which warrants may

[48] City of Dayton *v.* Board of Education of Dayton (Ky.), 205 S. W. 678; Eddy *v.* Wilson, 143 Vt. 365.

[49] People *v.* Bates, 107 N. E. (Ill.) 123; Board of Education of Bowling Green *v.* Townsend, 140 Ky. 248.

[50] Smithberg *v.* Archer, 108 Iowa 215.

[51] Morrell Refrigerator Car Co. *v.* Commonwealth, 128 Ky. 447; Wells *v.* Board of Education, 20 W. Va. 157; Cincinnati R. Co. *v.* Commonwealth, 51 S. W. (Ky.) 568; Oliver *v.* Carsner, 39 Texas 396.

[52] School Dist. No. 127 *v.* School Dist. No. 45 of Reno County, 103 P. (Kan.) 126.

be drawn within the amount of such levy, though the money with which to pay the warrants may not have been collected and on hand? Yes, it has been so held.[53]

Are taxes levied by one board collectible by a succeeding board? Since a school district is a corporation, it has a separate entity apart from its officers, and is therefore a continuous body. This answers the question in the affirmative and removes all doubt regarding the assessment and collection of taxes levied by a preceding board.[54] This assumes, of course, that the levy by the prior board is wholly legal.

May the board of education base its estimate of revenue which is needed to run the school on its previous experience and levy an additional amount to cover the loss of funds due to inability to collect some of the tax? Unless there is express statutory authority for so doing, a board of education cannot levy a larger amount than is actually needed in order to provide for the contingency of uncollected taxes.[55] The proper and legal procedure in such cases is through that provided by statute whereby delinquent taxes may be collected through the channel of sale of the property against which the taxes have been levied.

May public school property be assessed for local improvements? It may by express legislative authority, not otherwise. In St. Louis County *v.* Board of Education of City of Duluth,[56] Justice Hallam said:

> We hold in accordance with what seems to us the better reason as well as the weight of authority, that general laws subjecting property to the payment of assessments for local improvements do not apply to property devoted to use of the public schools, unless the intent that they do apply is made to affirmatively appear. . . .

May a tax levy be rescinded? This may be done at a regular or special election as provided by law, unless the tax has in the meantime been certified or actually levied.[57]

May a board of education levy taxes on property not subject to the general tax laws of the state? Unless by express legisla-

[53] Bank *v.* School Dist., 102 Kan. 98; Zimmerman *v.* State. 60 Neb. 633.
[54] Pond *v.* Negus, 3 Mass. 230.
[55] Board of Education of Newport *v.* City of Newport (Ky.), 171 Ky. 234.
[56] 158 N. W. (Minn.) 635.
[57] Kirchner *v.* Wapsinonoc School Township, 141 Iowa 43.

tive authority, this cannot be done. The designation of property to be taxed is an exclusive constitutional or legislative function and cannot be assumed by the taxing officers of the school district.[58] Numerous decisions point to the fact that taxable property is to be assessed the same for school purposes as for other governmental subdivisions. The legislature, however, may designate that certain property shall be assesssed for school purposes or that other property shall not be assessed. But in some states a school district may assess property at a different rate for school purposes than it is assessed for other purposes.[59] It all depends upon the will of the legislature.

Summary

1. Levy and assessment are indispensable to a valid tax. The former is legislative, the latter quasi-judicial.
2. If certain prerequisites are demanded before the levy and assessment may be made, they must be strictly observed.
3. The validity of a tax levy is not generally vitiated by mere irregularities that do not work injury to the taxpayer.
4. The time of levy is generally held to be directory and a slight delay will not invalidate the tax.
5. Taxes levied in excess of the statutory limit are void only as to such excess, unless the illegal cannot be separated from the legal tax.
6. The taxpayer has legal grounds for bringing an action against a board of education for an excessive levy of taxes and for any fraudulent act in connection with the levy therefor.
7. Taxes levied constitute a fund against which warrants may be drawn although the money may not be on hand with which to pay the warrants.
8. The right of boards of education to demand a back assessment of omitted property is unquestioned.

[58] State *v.* Gracey, 11 Nev. 223; Chadwick *v.* Crapsey, 35 N. Y. 196; Stephens *v.* School Dist. No. 21, 6 Or. 353; Glass *v.* Billings, 53 P. 125, 59 Kan. 776.

[59] Cooper *v.* Avery, 168 S. W. (Tex.) 412; *see also* 180 S. W. (Tex.) 734.

CHAPTER VI

PAYMENT AND COLLECTION OF THE TAX

Payment of taxes is not always made to school districts directly but to other authorized agencies for the collection of taxes in general. In many states the county treasurer receives the taxes, in others some lower court may be given the responsibility, while in others private institutions, such as banks, have been designated as tax collection agencies. There are, however, many legal questions surrounding tax collection which are germane to this study and therefore demand treatment.

It is frequently contended by taxpayers that the collection of the tax may be enjoined because all the property in the district subject to taxation has not been assessed. While it is a fundamental principle of taxation that all taxable property should pay its proportionate share of the tax burden for the support of schools, the fact that some property has been omitted from the tax list should not and does not invalidate the tax on the remaining property. The proper and legal proceeding is to start action for assessment of omitted property, or mandamus to compel the proper officer to furnish a complete list of all taxable property.[1]

Another prolific source of litigation to prevent the collection of school taxes is that of claiming irregularities in the proceedings relative to levy and assessment. Particularly is this true where certain taxpayers, such as large corporations, wish to reduce or to completely avoid payment of the amount of taxes assessed against them. While the statutes and the courts of the several states are not in agreement on what are mandatory and what are directory acts to be performed by a board of education in levying taxes, mere irregularities not affecting the validity of the tax are insufficient to cause a court to restrain a collection of the tax.[2]

[1] Creech *v.* Board of Trustees of Common School Dist. No. 15, 102 S. W. (Ky.) 804.

[2] Gray *v.* Board of Education of School Inspectors of Peoria, 83 N. E. 95, 231 Ill. 63.

When a taxpayer objects to the collection of a tax for any reason, the burden of proof showing why such a tax should not be collected is upon his shoulders. It is presumed that the officers of the district and those responsible for extending the tax on the rolls have performed their duties faithfully. So where an objector to a tax for educational purposes contends that part of the fund is to be used for building purposes, not the board of education, but the objector, must furnish proof of such unwarranted use.[3] When it is claimed that school property is used for other than school purposes and as such is a misapplication of the funds, it falls upon the claimant to show that the board of education has not the power under the law to devote the property to the uses in question.

There is no authority for requiring a school district to accept the tender of less than the amount of the taxes due from a taxpayer as a compromise settlement.[4] In case the tax has been adjudged excessive or illegally levied or assessed, entirely different proceedings are to be instituted for its final adjustment. If illegally levied or assessed, the tax should be set aside and legal proceedings carried out. If the rate or the valuation is excessive, resort to some board of equalization is generally the proper proceeding.

Delinquent Taxes

Since the taxing power "when acting within its legitimate sphere, is one which knows no stopping place, until it has accomplished the purpose for which it exists,"[5] ample provisions have been made in the tax laws for following the tax until it has been collected. It does not fall to the officers of school districts to initiate proceedings for delinquent taxes unless (1) they are directly interested in their own loss due to failure to collect the taxes, or (2) the tax in question is peculiarly a school tax. Boards of education pursue no different course in forcing the collection of delinquent taxes than do other governmental bodies. The legislature prescribes the steps that must be taken.

[3] People *v.* Meyer, 313 Ill. 332.

[4] Garza Land & Cattle Co. *v.* Redwine Indep. School Dist., 282 S. W. (Tex.) 905; Stuart *v.* Thompson, 251 S. W. (Tex.) 277.

[5] Anderson *v.* Ritterbusch, 98 P. (Okla.) 1002.

Much litigation occurs over the failure of the tax collecting agency to remit the taxes to the board of education. It is within the power of school district officers to compel county and municipal authorities who collect school taxes to pay over the amount of such taxes. In some jurisdictions this may be done although the taxes have not yet been collected.[6]

The question of who is entitled to the interest on delinquent taxes is well settled. The interest on that portion of the delinquent tax due the school district properly belongs to the district because such interest is an incident of the principal. A city or county withholding such interest is liable to the district for it.[7] And it does not matter that the principal has previously been paid; the interest is still due and collectible. In like manner, a city or other agency, charged with the duty of collecting school taxes, which collects taxes and interest and fails to pay them over to the board of education, but uses the money in its own affairs, is chargeable with the interest on the whole sum during the time thus appropriated to its own use.

Recovery of Taxes Paid

A. By the Taxpayer from the District

The recovery of taxes paid by mistake in the wrong district is a matter of difficulty for the taxpayer. A few illustrations of the trend of court decisions will be convincing. In San Diego Land Co. *v.* La Presa School District,[8] a special school tax, assessed upon improvements described as a dam situated in a tract of land within the school district, the dam being in fact outside the district, after voluntary payment, was not recoverable by the taxpayer. His grounds for recovery were, that he by mistake had paid the tax in the wrong district. He was liable for his mistake and could not forward it as grounds for recovery of the tax.

Although the illegality of the tax is sufficient grounds for the recovery by the taxpayer of tax money paid, in Davis *v.* Board of Education of Community Consolidated School Dis-

[6] Wallendorf *v.* Cole, County Court Justices, 45 Mo. 228.

[7] City of New Orleans *v.* Fisher, 91 F. 574.

[8] 122 Cal. 98, 54 P. 528.

trict No. 115,[9] the decision is to the contrary. Justice Heard said in part in the progress of rendering the court's opinion:

> The declaration shows that the taxes were paid by the appellant to the county treasurer voluntarily and not under duress, and therefore he cannot recover back the money paid, although the tax may be illegal.[10]

Yet in Joyner *v.* Inhabitants of School District No. 3,[11] the contrary ruling is made. In this case, the inhabitants of a school district voted to raise money for building a schoolhouse. This money was assessed and collected and paid by the collector into the town treasury. It was then paid by the treasurer to a building committee appointed by the district. At this juncture the assessment was declared illegal and void. It was held that a taxpayer might recover the amount of money he had paid under this void assessment. The weight of authority leans to the rule that to warrant a recovery of money paid by mistake the tax must have been illegal and void and paid under protest. Where the objector has full access to the tax books and all facts pertaining to the tax, and pays voluntarily, he must bear the burden of showing that the tax was illegal. The mere matter of a mistake in paying the tax into the wrong district or having the property assessed in the wrong situs will not warrant a recovery of the tax.

It is not uncommon for school trustees to supplement school funds by their own private means when a deficit is impending, expecting to recoup themselves from tax moneys at a later period. This is a dangerous thing to do. While such an act is to be highly commended as public-spirited, the difficulties surrounding the recovery of funds so temporarily lent the district are too hazardous to be undertaken. While it is possible and lawful to recoup themselves from funds remaining after all expenditures are paid, the public, no matter how laudably it may approve the generosity of the board in the first instance, is too quick to cast an eye of suspicion upon the second part of the

[9] 154 N. E. 127, 323 Ill. 281.

[10] *See also* Conkling *v.* City of Springfield, 132 Ill. 420; Bradford *v.* City of Chicago, 25 Ill. 349; U. P. R. Co. *v.* Dodge County Commissioners, 98 U. S. 541.

[11] 57 Mass. 567.

act.[12] The better procedure in such instances is to borrow funds through legitimate channels.

B. One District from Another

Indistinct and poorly defined school district boundaries, frequent change of assessors, and transfer of ownership of property all contribute to assessment of property in the wrong district. First, let us set forth the principle with reference to recovery by one district of tax moneys after it has been set off from its original district into another or separate district. The same rule is applicable as in the section, "Time at Which Situs for Taxation Becomes Fixed." Taxes levied for the construction of a schoolhouse or for other expenses of a district, a subsequent partition of the territory of the district being made, does not relieve the taxpayers so set off into another district from the obligation of paying the tax levied on the original district.[13] Conversely, a part of the territory of a district set off before such levy was consummated cannot be compelled to pay over any tax money on the taxable property in its own district to the district from which it has been set off.

The second principle of general acceptance is, that where one school district collects by mistake taxes on property in another district, the latter, if any recovery can be made, can recover no more than the amount it would have received without the mistake.[14] If the rate of taxation be higher in the district in which the property is erroneously taxed than in the other, the amount recoverable will be that raised by the levy in the district in which the property actually was situated. The excess due to the higher rate cannot be recovered. Taxes levied on property in the wrong district are with difficulty recovered after they have been collected, distributed to the district, and consumed for educational purposes.[15] But in many states legislation has made provision for such refund, an example of which is Kansas. In a case

[12] Flanders *v.* Board of Trustees of Little Rock Graded School, 186 S. W. 506, 170 Ky. 627.

[13] Dyer *v.* School Dist. No. 1, 61 Vt. 96, 17 A. 788.

[14] Walser *v.* Board of Education, 160 Ill. 272, 43 N. E. 346.

[15] Mabelvale Special School Dist. *v.* Halstead Special School Dist., 276 S. W. (Ark.) 584.

of recent settlement,[16] where by mistake property in one district was listed as being in another, and without knowledge of the error taxes were paid, and distributed to the two districts and used for school purposes, it was ruled that the district thus losing the tax could recover a sum equal to the amount it would have received if its levy had been extended against the property erroneously listed. A contrary, but earlier, decision in Illinois [17] is to the effect that the tax money collected from property assessed in one district cannot be recovered by the district of actual situs of the property on the grounds of mistake or error in the district map. It is evident from the above discussion that the courts are not agreed as to the grounds essential to a recovery of taxes on property assessed by one district but located in another, beyond the very general principle laid down at the beginning of the paragraph.

Proceedings to Enforce Collection

It is not within the scope of this study to include all the proceedings relative to enforcement of tax collection. Only in rare cases does the board of education have the power to proceed directly against the delinquent taxpayer. This power must be expressly granted by legislative enactment. Inasmuch as tax collection is carried out by means of a separate agency—which is accountable for all taxes on the list or warrant—the school board's action for enforcement of return of tax moneys is against such collector. The collector is accountable for not only the taxes he has collected but also for those he might have collected by diligent effort and by the employment of whatever legal remedies are within his authority.[18] As previously stated, he must turn over not only the tax but the interest and whatever penalties are attached for delayed payment.

The tax collector, however, may have justifiable excuses for having failed to collect the tax and may use any one or all of

[16] School Dist. No. 8, etc., *v.* Board of Education of Kansas City, 224 P. (Kan.) 892. *See also* 162 Iowa 42.

[17] School Directors Dist. No. 153 *v.* School Directors Dist. No. 154, 232 Ill. 322; *see also* Walser *v.* Board of Education of School Dist. No. 1, 160 Ill. 572.

[18] Fidelity, etc., Co. *v.* Mobile County, 124 Ala. 144, 27 So. 386; Gorham *v.* Hall, 57 Me. 58.

them as defenses in an action against him. His best defenses are:

1. The unconstitutionality of the statute under which the levy or the assessment or both were made.[19]
2. A defective or insufficient warrant for collection.[20]
3. The fact that he was enjoined by a court of law from the collection of the tax.
4. Removal from office before sufficient time had elapsed for collection to be made.

It is obvious that tax collection cannot be enforced under an unconstitutional statute. New laws in conflict with old, and new legislation passed with the intent of meeting changed conditions in conflict with statutes passed without consideration of such changed conditions, produce many cases of unconstitutionality in the tax statutes. Until such defects are cured by subsequent legislation, the tax collector is powerless to proceed with tax collection. A warrant for tax collection may be defective in several ways. It may require that an affirmative vote of the electors of the district be shown for levying the tax; it may be defective in the assessment, such as an improper or indistinct description of property. The power of injunction may be employed to prevent tax collection under unusual conditions demanding a stay of the collector's hand until some apparent difficulty may be righted, or permanently, in the case of an unlawful tax. But it must be borne in mind that the collector has no defense that taxes were unlawfully levied if he has collected them.[21]

It is well settled that the capacity to sue for and recover school moneys from a collector is in the officers who have the authority to receive and disburse such funds,[22] namely, the board of education through its treasurer. That education is a state function permits the local board of education in many instances to bring action in the name of the state.[23] This adds dignity and weight

[19] Boring *v.* Williams, 17 Ala. 510.

[20] State *v.* Rushing, 17 Fla. 226.

[21] O'Neal *v.* Washington County School Commissioners, 27 Md. 227.

[22] *Supra,* note 21; Stokes County Board of Education *v.* Wall, 117 N. C. 382, 23 S. E. 358.

[23] *Supra,* note 21; Tappan *v.* People, 67 Ill. 339; State *v.* Kelley, 43 Tex. 667.

to the school board's case and also gives an opportunity for the employment of expert counsel.

The methods possible for compelling the collector to make collection and return of tax moneys are (1) mandamus, (2) assumpsit, and (3) action on his official bond against him and his sureties.[24]

In O'Neal *v.* Board of School Commissioners of Washington County (Md.), Justice Bartol emphasizes the board's right to demand moneys collected, in the following excerpt from the opinion of the court:

> Here the proof shows that the levy . . . was made by the County Commissioners for the use of the school fund. . . . He [collector] assumed the duty of making collection for the uses indicated; and when money was received by him, it enured to the use of the Commissioners who by law were entitled to demand and receive the school fund.

Collectors generally gather all the taxes within their jurisdiction—state, county, and local. Where such is the case, they may sell property for delinquent school taxes even though the other taxes have been paid.[25] But it is beyond a collector's power to sell the whole of a tract of land where part of it lies outside the district claiming the delinquent tax.[26] While in some states, land in one body owned by the same person, but lying in more than one school district, is assessed for taxes in but one of the districts, sale of the whole tract for delinquent taxes would involve a crossing of district boundaries—an action not contemplated by the statute. Unless the statutes of limitations apply expressly to delinquent taxes, the lapse of time does not prevent a state or its political subdivisions from collecting delinquent taxes.[27] Statutes to the contrary may be enacted by the lawmaking body and in some jurisdictions have been so enacted.

Assumed Defenses of the Taxpayer. As in every action at law, both parties have real or assumed grounds for defense. The delinquent taxpayer always has an excuse for nonpayment. Whether the excuse matured into a real defense depends upon it

[24] *See also* Allhands *v.* People, 82 Ill. 234; *supra,* note 21; Sunapee School Dist. No. 8 *v.* Perkins, 49 N. H. 538.

[25] Ogden City *v.* Hamer, 12 Utah 337, 42 P. 1113.

[26] Shaw *v.* Lockett, 14 Colo. App. 413, 60 P. 363.

[27] San Francisco *v.* Jones, 20 F. 188; Hogan *v.* Ingle, 12 Fed. Cas. No. 6583

and upon the law of the commonwealth. Some of the common defenses for nonpayment of taxes are:

1. That there was want of authority on the part of the collector to gather the tax.
2. That his property was exempt.
3. That he had already paid the tax.
4. That he had no interest in the property at the time of levy and assessment of the tax.
5. That the tax levy or assessment contained an element of fraud.
6. That no election was held to authorize the tax (where an election is required).
7. That the title to land upon which a school building is to be erected is clouded.
8. That he had a claim for damages against the district as a set-off for a part or all of the taxes.
9. That he did not enter the district as a property owner in time to participate in the election for trustees.
10. That he had no opportunity to participate in the election authorizing the tax.
11. That there were inequalities in the assessment.
12. That he was taxed in the wrong situs.
13. That the district was unorganized at the time of levy.

Let us see how many of the assumed defenses are real in the general application of the statutes. If the taxpayer can show that the collector was without authority, he may resist payment successfully. It is necessary that every collector be clothed with power and possess the required authority to legally collect the taxes.[28] A failure to be properly chosen for the office; failure to furnish the required bond; and failure to qualify as to other requirements may leave the collector without authority to proceed in his duty. Objection on the grounds of property exemption must be proved by the objector. No property is exempt unless the statutes expressly provide therefor. That he purchased property formerly exempt, does not relieve him from taxation on the property unless the same conditions prevail as

[28] Odem *v.* Sinton Indep. School Dist., 234 S. W. (Tex.) 1090.

before purchase. If the property owner can objectively show that he has paid the tax, he is relieved from further payment during the same year. But he must have proof of payment to support his case.

That a delinquent taxpayer had no interest in the property at the time of levy and assessment does not necessarily relieve him from payment of the tax thereon. If he purchased the property and the title passed after the tax date or after assessment, it is his own fault if he did not have included in the sale contract that all previous and assessed taxes were to be paid. However, under certain circumstances it is possible for the purchaser of property after the assessment date to rest the burden of taxes on the original owner. Much depends upon the contract between them. If an element of fraud can be shown in the proceedings for levying and assessing the tax, the tax becomes void and all taxpayers are absolved from obligation to pay. But the burden of showing such fraudulent actions is upon the taxpayer.[29] If an election is by statute required for authorizing a tax, it is a defense to maintain that none was held, for such defect will invalidate the tax.

One cannot resist the collection of a school tax on the ground that the title to the land on which the building is to be erected is defective so long as the possession is not disturbed.[30] But action to contest the title may be set up as a defense. The fact that a taxpayer has a claim against the school district does not warrant him nor furnish him a defense for attempting to set off his claim against the district's claim for taxes. The two claims are of entirely different nature, and actions for their satisfaction are under different proceedings. The property owner's claim, if he has one, is likely to be based on contract and can be pursued only by the legal methods provided for compelling fulfillment of such contract. Taxes are not contracts, but obligations demanded by a sovereign power for the support of government. He may sue the school district for his claim, but may not set it off against due and accrued taxes.[31]

A property owner may enter a district as such before the as-

[29] Common School Dist. No. 88 *v.* Garvey, 80 Ky. 159.

[30] People *v.* Sisson, 93 Ill. 335.

[31] McCracken *v.* Elder, 34 Pa. St. 239.

sessment date but after the election of members of the board who certify the tax. Or he may be prohibited from voting for them under a presumption that he is outside the district or for other reasons. But these incidental facts have no effect to release him from taxation on the property he owns within the school district.[32] In like manner, he may become a property owner in a school district after a tax has been authorized by vote of the people in the district, but before the tax has been actually levied on the taxable property of the district. His lack of opportunity to participate in such election is no defense for refusal to pay taxes.

Inequalities in the assessment cannot be set up as a defense for nonpayment of taxes unless it can be shown that there was fraud connected therewith. The proper body to correct unequal assessments is a board of equalization or some similar body empowered to adjust assessment claims.[33] As to taxation in the wrong situs, the statutes and decisions are at variance, some declaring that taxation of property in the wrong situs invalidates the whole assessment. Others hold that the tax may be recovered; while still others rule that an erroneous payment in one political subdivision does not discharge a valid assessment for taxation in another.[34] Therefore, it may be stated that taxation in the wrong situs as a defense to failure to pay taxes may be maintained in some jurisdictions and not in others, depending upon the nature of the case and the statutes in force. No general rule, therefore, can be set up to answer this question.

An organized school district is an entity separate from its officers who compose the body corporate for the transaction of the district's business. Delegation of the authority to tax must be made to an organized political subdivision capable of acting in a legislative capacity. It follows, therefore, that if he can prove the lack of organization of the district, a taxpayer may use such fact to substantiate his refusal to pay taxes. So a tax is illegal if the board has been ousted [35] and no de facto board is provided for transacting the business of the district.

[32] Grout *v.* Illingworth, 108 N. W. 528, 131 Iowa 281.
[33] State *v.* Cunningham, 153 Mo. 642.
[34] Beal-Dayle Dry Goods Co. *v.* Beller, 150 S. W. 1033, 105 Ark. 370.
[35] People *v.* New York Central R. Co., 119 N. E. 299, 283 Ill. 334.

Summary

1. Delinquent taxes plus the interest thereon belong to the school district where levied for school purposes and legal action may be maintained against the collector to obtain them.

2. A taxpayer can with difficulty collect taxes paid into the wrong district unless he can support proof that some element of illegality entered into their levy, and that he paid them under duress.

(Recovery by one district of taxes erroneously paid in another depends upon the peculiar circumstances and the statutes in effect regarding such recovery.)

3. Unless he has justifiable grounds for noncollection of the tax, a collector may be, by proper legal means, compelled to collect such taxes.

4. The taxpayer has legal defenses for refusal to pay his taxes, but generally must bear the burden of showing that his defense is tenable. He may successfully claim that

a. He has paid the tax,
b. His property was exempt,
c. The collector was without authority to collect,
d. He had no interest in the property at time of levy,
e. The levy or assessment had an element of fraud,
f. No election (where required) was held, and
g. District was unorganized at time of levy.

He may not maintain an action that

a. Title to land for a school building was clouded,
b. He has a claim against district to offset the taxes,
c. He entered district too late to participate in the election for trustees or for the tax levy,
d. There were inequalities in the assessment, and
e. He was taxed in the wrong situs, unless statutes provide accordingly.

CHAPTER VII

RIGHTS AND REMEDIES OF TAXPAYERS

In Erroneous Taxation

This study deals primarily with the rights and liabilities of school boards with respect to taxation. But it is impossible to divorce the taxpayer from consideration, as has been seen throughout the progress of the study. The board's liability may at times be the taxpayer's prerogative. If the board of education is responsible to the taxpayer for the performance of certain duties, that performance becomes a legal right of the taxpayer. The two are inseparable in a complete development of the study of taxation. In the previous chapters the board of education has been the object of our consideration. This chapter attempts to outline in brief some rights of the taxpayer on his own account, together with the chief remedies he has for enforcement of his rights against the board of education in particular.

Notwithstanding the multiplicity—perhaps because of it—of the laws regulating the assessment and collection of taxes for school purposes, a large amount of litigation develops not only between outside interests and the schools but also between taxpayer and the board of education. Each has rights which must be respected and if not respected, resort to the courts is the proper remedy. It is not singular that the difficulties between board and property owner are seldom concerned with too little taxation, reduction of valuation and rate; but with the levy when it becomes noticeable to the one who supports the public burden.

The chief type of legal action the taxpayer brings against the board of education is that one wherein he prays to prevent a tax from being collected. He may base his case upon illegal levy or assessment, but since the collection of the tax is the only proceeding which directly affects him, he throws his weight of legal right against its enforcement. Occasionally, the suit may be brought to prevent the levy, as where taxpaying citizens sue to restrain the school board from levying taxes to pay interest on illegal bonds. It is well settled that a taxpayer has the right to institute an action to restrain the board of education from doing an illegal act.[1]

Injunction is a frequently employed legal means of controlling the power of boards of education in matters of taxation in order to protect the rights of the taxpayer. Injunction is not granted, however, where there are other remedies at law. When so granted it must be used in strict conformity with statutory inhibitions. It will lie to restrain the assessment and collection of illegal school taxes. Such illegality may arise from making the levy without authority or upon property not taxable within the district.[2] The proper method of restraining taxation beyond the statutory limits is by injunction. In the following cases it may not be employed:

1. To restrain the collection of the tax merely because of irregularities in the proceedings of the taxing officers.[3]
2. To interfere with the discretion of the taxing officers in the absence of fraud.[4]
3. Where it does not appear that a taxpayer has been injured in his property rights or that such rights are in danger.[5]
4. To prevent a proposed diversion of funds. (Court of equity may do this after the tax has been collected.)
5. To set aside the tax because certain things are done within the school system different than prescribed by law.[6]
6. Because of misunderstandings between the voters and the officers about the location of a proposed building.[7]

In the following allegations, injunction will lie to restrain a board of education:

[1] Youmans *v.* Board of Education, 13 Ohio Cir. R. 207.

[2] Simpkins *v.* Ward, 8 N. W. 507, 45 Mich. 559; Roberts *v.* Murphy, 86 S. E. 545, 144 Ga. 177; Brown *v.* Hawkins, 77 S. E. 1123, 139 Ga. 697; *Same v.* Horne, 77 S. E. 1125, 139 Ga. 702.

[3] Munson *v.* Minor, 22 Ill. 594; State *v.* Bremond, 38 Ill. 116; Travelstead *v.* Ray, 185 S. W. 91.

[4] Wharton *v.* Cass Tp. School Directors, 42 Pa. St. 358.

[5] Lagow *v.* Hill, 143 Ill. App. 523.

[6] Richards *v.* Raymond, 92 Ill. 612.

[7] Jones *v.* Coleman, 111 S. E. 377, 152 Ga. 795.

1. Where it appears that the tax levied will exceed the statutory limit.
2. In cases where it appears that the board has acted without authority of law, such as relocating a schoolhouse.[8]
3. Arbitrary and excessive valuation of property for school assessment over that for state and county purposes without regard to market value.[9]
4. An attempt to collect an illegal tax.[10]
5. A levy containing an element of fraud.
6. Assessment and levy of property outside the district boundaries.[11]

It has been stated that injunction will not be granted where other legal remedies are available. After an act has been done, injunction is of no avail for it acts to prevent the commission of an apparently unauthorized or illegal act. After the tax has been collected, the proper legal remedy to prevent its being devoted to purposes foreign to those for which it was levied, is a suit in equity. For example, in the case of a high school district which had selected a site for a building and had invested $15,000 in the schoolhouse, but soon voted to purchase a new site because of the spitework of certain electors, equity has jurisdiction in a taxpayer's suit to require that the board proceed with the original construction. The taxpayer here has the right to a legal remedy because he is able to show that the purchase of the new and the abandonment of the old site will result in a waste of his and other taxpayers' money.[12] In a different situation, however, a taxpayer cannot maintain an action to compel a board to do or not to do an act clearly within the board's discretion. For example, the courts will not intervene to prevent a school district board from employing a certain person as super-

[8] Wall-Hay-Wall Lumber Co. *v.* Mathews, 100 So. (Ala.) 824; Kellogg *v.* School Dist. No. 10 of Comanche County, 74 P. (Okla.) 110; McLain *v.* Maricle, 83 N. W. 85, 60 Neb. 353; Hysler *v.* Board of Education, 201 Ill. App. 116.

[9] Power *v.* Andrews, 253 S. W. (Tex.) 870.

[10] *Supra,* note 2; State *v.* Mad River Tp. Rural School Dist., 104 Ohio St. 360.

[11] *Supra,* note 2.

[12] Allred *v.* Dunn, 93 So. (Ala.) 390; Moss *v.* Board of Education of Special School Dist. No. 1, 921 Ohio St. 354; Iverson *v.* Union Free High School Dist., etc., 202 N. W. 788, 186 Wis. 342; Hysler *v.* Board of Education of Springfield School Dist. No. 186, 201 Ill. App. 116, judgment affirmed 112 N. E. 414.

intendent or as teacher.[13] Again, where an action at law would affect an innocent party, it cannot be maintained, as, for example, a suit to restrain the levy of taxes to pay bonds where the bonds had been issued and transferred to a third party.[14]

In the collection of illegal school taxes where property has been taken to compel payment of the tax, the taxpayer may recover not only the amount of the tax he has been compelled to pay, but also the amount it has cost him to redeem his property.[15] The action maintained is one of trespass for illegal seizure of property. The taxpayer must constantly keep in mind the fact that upon him falls the burden of proof in all action seeking to enjoin a levy or collection of taxes on the grounds of void election, unauthorized tax, excess of legal limit, and other unlawful proceedings.[16]

Personal and Estoppel Rights

The right of a resident of one school district to have his children transferred to another district and his taxes paid to the second district cannot be denied him on the grounds that withdrawal of his taxes from the former district will lay a heavier burden upon the remaining property owners. If he is within his right, the question of the tax will not prevent such transfer. Transfer is usually granted for the advantage of the children who attend school and no question of a slightly heavier burden on other taxpayers should operate to deprive them of an increased advantage.[17] Residents of a school district living outside the limits of a town, although still in the district, cannot claim illegality of the tax imposed on them simply because all of the district officers live within the city limits. It is not taxation without representation, because the district is not confined to the city limits and board members have power to levy and collect taxes over the whole district.[18]

[13] Jensen *v.* Indep. Consol. School Dist. No. 85, etc., 199 N. W. (Minn.) 911.

[14] Lerew *v.* Cresbard Indep. Consol. School Dist. No. 2, etc., 192 N. W. (S. D.) 747.

[15] Tucker *v.* Wentworth, 35 Me. 393.

[16] O'Loughlin *v.* Dorn, 169 N. W. (Wis.) 572; Glover's Guardian *v.* Common School Dist., 14 Ky. L. Rep. 240; Weeks *v.* Hetland, 202 N. W. (N. D.) 807.

[17] A. O. U. W. *v.* Paragould Special School Dist. No. 1, 222 S. W. (Ark.) 368.

[18] Morris *v.* Smith, 112 S. E. (Ga.) 468.

A few illustrations of a taxpayer's estoppel rights will reveal the underlying principles. Where a taxpayer attended a meeting of a school district in which he resided, to determine the rate of tax to be levied for the support of schools, and made a motion at the meeting, he was estopped to deny the regularity of the proceedings.[19] Where the acts of school trustees in creating an indebtedness and levying a tax to pay it are void, taxpayers are not estopped by the fact that they had notice of the creation of the debt and paid the tax without complaint for two years.[20] Evidence that an alderman voted for an ordinance levying a school tax was sufficient to authorize a finding that he was estopped from resisting collection of the tax after the expense of nearly an entire term of school had been incurred in reliance on the tax.[21] The examination of other similar cases warrants deduction of the following principles: (1) that the taxpayer, even though he has participated in the proceedings to establish the tax and even has paid it without complaint, is not estopped to question its validity in the face of reasonable evidence that it may be illegal; (2) that the taxpayer is estopped from denying the regularity of proceedings to which he was a party.

Disposition of the Proceeds of the Tax

This division of the study does not contemplate in any way an analysis of the distribution of school funds on the bases commonly employed in school accounting. Nor does it pretend to cover all the legal school purposes for which funds raised by taxation may be expended. There is seldom any disagreement or misunderstanding over the board of education's power to erect buildings wherewith to house the children of the district. Furthermore, the legal implications of this phase have been admirably set forth in another study.[22] No one contests the board's power to employ teachers and pay their salaries out of

[19] Martin *v.* School Dist. of Town of Lawrence, 35 S. E. 517, 57 S. C. 125.

[20] Howard *v.* Trustees of School Dist. No. 27, 1025 S. W. 318; Loesche *v.* Goerdt, 123 Iowa 55.

[21] Burkhart *v.* City of Fitzgerald, 73 S. E. 583; *see also* Wood *v.* Calaveras County, 164 Cal. 398.

[22] Henzlik, F. E. *Rights and Liabilities of Public School Boards under Capital Outlay Contracts.* Bureau of Publications, Teachers College, Columbia University, 1924.

public revenue. This phase is also treated in a separate study dealing with the legal status of the teacher.[23] What is contemplated here is an organization of those principles of law which guide the courts in their adjudication of cases arising under the statutes, pertaining to the use of tax-raised funds when the legality of the use is in question.

Since education is a function of the state, all school funds properly are state funds in the final analysis. This is true until some person acquires a vested right to such funds. There is no question that funds to maintain public schools are for a public purpose. Yet it is obvious from the amount of litigation over the use of school funds that there is much misunderstanding of what a public purpose is. There are also frequent attempts to divert the funds raised for a specific purpose to some other purpose.

Returning to the principle that taxes can be levied for only public purposes, we are admonished to remember that "public use extends far beyond the mere denial of the right to collect a tax which has been levied for a private purpose. The right to tax depends upon the ultimate use, purpose, and object for which the fund is raised."[24] Appropriations of money out of the school fund must be measured by the same test as that required for levying of the tax to put it into the treasury. "If taxes could not be imposed for a purpose, money already in the treasury could not be appropriated to that purpose."[25] It must also be recognized that the same principle makes it unlawful for any governmental body to undertake an enterprise which may involve the expenditure of money unless it is a public enterprise, even though no tax has been or is anticipated to be levied in aid of it. Failure of such enterprise would necessitate the employment of taxation to pay the debt incurred.[26]

What constitutes a public purpose is not easy to determine. Such determination must be made in the light of present practice, established custom, and the objects for which taxes are generally

[23] Allen, I. N. *Contractual Status of the Teacher.* Bureau of Publications, Teachers College, Columbia University, 1928.

[24] Sharpless *v.* Philadelphia, 21 Pa. St. 147.

[25] Hager *v.* Ky. Children's Home Society, 119 Ky. 235, 83 S. W. 605.

[26] State *v.* Lynch, 88 Ohio St. 71; Mahon *v.* Board of Education, 171 N. Y. 263.

levied to support the schools of the nation. The line is generally drawn close as shown in a recent case [27] in New York State. This case arose over the printing of cards for a denominational institution by a public school on material belonging to the board of education. The decision was to the effect that the board of education had violated a constitutional prohibition against using its property, funds, or credit in aid of a religious denominational school. Not even the charitable nature of a private or denominational school will entitle it to receive public funds in aid of its support in most jurisdictions. Only those schools over which the state has ultimate control can profit from the use of public revenue.[28] It has been held that the permission to use the public schools for certain exercises by religious bodies and private religious institutions of learning is not under certain conditions a violation of the principle of "public funds for public use." But there are contrary decisions with good authority to sustain them.

Boards of education are not permitted under the statutes of some states even to contract to send children to a private school at a tuition charge even though the public schools are unable to temporarily accommodate such children.

Illegal Disposition of Funds. Any misappropriation of the school funds entrusted to school district officers is illegal. This paragraph relates to those principles where illegality is the issue and not some other use of the fund. It is a fundamental principle that a taxpayer may maintain an action to prevent an illegal disposition of public school money or the illegal creation of a debt which he, in common with other taxpayers, may be compelled to pay.[29] But the mere proposed diversion of the collected tax to a foreign purpose will not sustain an action. In like manner where taxes have been paid for school purposes without objection, their use for the purposes for which they were levied will not be prevented by any mere technical objections as to the manner in which the levy was made.[30] It is an illegal disposition of the school tax to devote a certain per cent of it

[27] Stein *v.* Brown, 211 N. Y. S. 822.

[28] Curtis *v.* Whipple, 24 Wis. 350; Otken *v.* Lamkin, 26 Miss. 758; Underwood *v.* Wood, 93 Ky. 177.

[29] Kellogg *v.* School Dist. No. 10 of Comanche County, 74 P. (Okla.) 110; Greer *v.* Austin, 40 Okla. 113; Sugar *v.* Monroe, 108 La. 677.

[30] Trustees of School *v.* Board of School Inspectors, 115 Ill. App. 479.

to sinking fund purposes for the town or city school bonds when the district is not coterminous with the city limits, as taking property without due process of law from those outside the city or town limits. This decision was reached in a case wherein the territory outside the town limits was not a portion of the town district when the bonds were issued and was therefore not liable on them unless so agreed on extension of the district. It is not an illegal disposition of a school fund for common schools to use a portion of it to pay tuition for its high school pupils who have been required to attend a high school district.[31] The non-resident taxpayer has the right to an action to compel the proper expenditure of school funds by the board of education, although not residing in the district.[32]

Misuse of Funds Affecting Buildings and Sites. The execution of an illegal contract by the district board for the erection of a building may be prevented by an individual or corporate taxpayer. Unless otherwise forbidden by statute, a board of education may add money derived from taxation to that raised by a bond issue to build a schoolhouse.[33] This principle is based on the assumption that the money raised by taxation was for building purposes or that no restriction was placed upon it. In the event such equipment for a proposed building as a heating plant or electric and plumbing equipment are not specifically provided for in the school board's authorization to build a school building, the board is within its rights in using part of the fund for such equipment or in levying an additional tax to provide for it. This right was upheld in a carefully prepared decision,[34] reciting that since such equipment is an indispensable part of school buildings the board of education cannot consistently perform their duty in erecting buildings without the coördinate power to equip them.

Frequently action is brought to restrain a school board from purchasing a site upon which to erect a proposed building on the grounds that the purpose for which the tax was levied did not include such expenditure. But the weight of authority grants

[31] Board of Education, etc., *v.* Tuttle, 211 N. Y. S. 413.
[32] Case *v.* Blood, 71 Iowa 632, 33 N. W. 144.
[33] Gaddis *v.* School Dist. of City of Lincoln, 139 N. W. 280, 92 Neb. 701.
[34] St. Louis, etc., R. Co. *v.* People, 79 N. E. 664, 224 Ill. 155.

a board of education the power to acquire a site for the building, since the acquisition of land is a necessary precedent to the erection of the building.[35] But, on the other hand, money raised by a tax to provide a building cannot be diverted to other uses,[36] such as to maintain schools or to transport pupils. Where the law provides for separate funds for building and for general educational purposes, each fund "is earmarked with a trust for the particular purpose and cannot be commingled or used interchangeably." [37]

Transfer of Funds. It has already been stated that building and educational funds cannot be interchanged. What about the specific purpose for which other funds are raised? Much depends upon the law in the particular state. Where the law provides that maintenance and operation funds are specific, they cannot be used for building purposes.[38] It is quite commonly impossible for a board of education to divert taxes levied for current expenses to pay indebtedness created during a previous year.[39] Some jurisdictions do not prohibit such practice. In Missouri, money collected by taxation for school purposes cannot be diverted from one fund to another—such as transfer of teachers' fund money to the incidentals fund.[40] Some states do not forbid the practice of transfer of funds [41] of this nature.

Most of the Southern states provide that funds set apart for schools for white children cannot be used for schools in which colored children are educated, even after the funds in the latter district have been exhausted.[42]

Salaries and Commissions of Collectors. Practice, based upon statute, as to the payment of tax collectors' salaries out of school revenue is not uniform. In states where the county treasurer or municipal tax collector gathers the tax and is paid a salary for that and other duties, commissions on collected taxes are not

[35] Knopf *v.* People, 185 Ill. 20, 57 N. E. 22.

[36] Gibson *v.* Anderson, 186 S. W. 497, 170 Ky. 664; People *v.* Chicago, etc., Ry. Co., 133 N. E. (Ill.) 339.

[37] Knopf *v.* People, 185 Ill. 20, 57 N. E. 22.

[38] Riesen *v.* School Dist. No. 4, 212 N. W. 783, 192 Wis. 283.

[39] Gulf Pipe Line Co. *v.* County Treasurer of Tulsa County, 236 P. 896, 11 Okla. 163.

[40] Cleveland, etc., Dist. No. 118 *v.* Zion, 190 S. W. (Mo.) 955.

[41] Stinson *v.* Thorson, 158 N. W. (N. D.) 351.

[42] Jones *v.* Board of Education, etc., 217 P. 400, 90 Okla. 233.

common and therefore not deducted from any fund. But where tax collection is performed on a commission basis, the question arises as to whether school taxes must bear their proportion of collection charges. In County Board of Education *v.* Austin [43] it was held that it is not a diversion of school funds to deduct from them the just proportion of salaries of county treasurer and collector. But in City of Winchester *v.* Board of Education of City of Winchester [44] the school board's acquiescence in payment of the tax collector's commissions out of taxes collected for school purposes did not estop the board from asserting in an action therefor its right to the amount deducted from school taxes for such purposes during past years. No general rule can be laid down for such use of school funds except to say that it is not a diversion of school funds to pay the collector's salary or commission where the law provides that he be paid in that manner.

The Payment of Tuition. While the payment of tuition is recognized in most states as a legitimate use of public school funds, there are complications which often bring such use of school funds into the courts for settlement. The laws in most states require that a pupil who is not a resident of a school district is entitled to attend school therein only upon the payment of tuition. But the question of determining when a pupil is a bona fide resident is not so easily disposed of. The principle of most common application is that laid down in several Wisconsin cases.[45] They cite a long line of authority for their stand, all of which is supported by sound and reasonable judgment. Their rule is that where a child's primary purpose in coming into a school district is to attend the public schools of that place, he must pay tuition, although there is some incidental purpose to be served while he attends the school. If a child is sent or goes into a district for the express purpose of making that his home, he has residence there and is entitled to the privilege of attending school therein. Some states have more detailed and specific laws regulating the payment of tuition and the courts are obliged to

[43] 276 S. W. (Ark.) 2.

[44] 206 S. W. 492, 182 Ky. 313.

[45] State *ex rel* School Dist. No. 1 *v.* Thayer, 74 Wis. 48; State *v.* Eau Claire Board of Education, 96 Wis. 95, 71 N. W. 123; *see also* School Dist. v Bragdon, 23 N. H. 507: School Dist. *v.* Pollard, 55 N. H. 503.

make interpretations in the light of such regulatory laws. It may be stated as a matter of policy in all such matters that the child's side of the case carries the weight of evidence, other things being equal, for the state expects each child to have equal educational advantages. The spirit of the law will be observed rather than the letter in order to swing the balance in favor of the child.

Many children are presumed to have their domicile with their parents, but there are numerous exceptions. If domiciled with their parents they are not entitled to attend school without tuition in another district although they may have a more or less permanent home within that district.[46] Where it can be shown that the child has not been domiciled at the home of his parents for a period of years and that he is required to make his home with relatives or friends, such fact generally establishes a residence for school purposes.

No school district is liable for tuition for the attendance of a pupil in another district's high school when the former district has a high school of equal grade or after the pupil has graduated from a complete high school course.[47] Payment of such unauthorized tuition is an appropriation of school funds to an illegal purpose and may be restrained by proper action. Where it is impracticable or impossible to hold school in a district, it is possible to raise money by taxation to pay the tuition of the children of such district to attend in another district.[48] In some instances it is possible to even pay their transportation to such school, and in some states obligatory to do so.

Many states at this time have made provision for free high school tuition for those children living in districts not maintaining a high school. In some states the home district is liable for the tuition of such children; in others, the county is made the unit for a tax levy to defray such expense.

Selection of Site Outside Municipal Limits. We have spoken of the rule applicable to selection of a site upon which a school building is to be erected and the power to levy a tax for such

[46] Binde *v.* Klinge, 30 Mo. App. 285; *see also* Lacy *v.* Williams, 27 Mass. 280.
[47] New Hampton Institute *v.* Northwood School Dist., 74 N. H. 412, 68 Atl. 538.
[48] Associated School *v.* School Dist. No. 83, 122 Minn. 254, 142 N. W. 325.

purpose. The more regular locations of sites were then in mind. Is it a wrongful use of school funds for the board of education to select a site outside the limits of the city when school districts and city boundaries are coterminous? Several court decisions [49] uphold the right of the board to so select the site when conditions favoring that site are peculiar to the situation. The argument in the case of Reams *v.* Board of Mayor and Aldermen of McMinnville (Tenn.) is succinctly given in the opinion rendered by Justice Cook as follows:

> In the location and establishment of the school the mayor and aldermen were acting in the reasonable exercise of discretionary powers conferred upon them by statute, and they did not transcend their powers in selecting a site beyond, but near, the corporate limits of the town.

The board of mayor and aldermen act as a board of education in the case quoted above in selecting sites, erecting buildings, establishing schools, and maintaining them. It must be clearly kept in mind that only as the power to select sites is reposed in the board of education does it have any discretion as to where the site should be. Under many jurisdictions, the people, by vote, have a voice in the selection of schoolhouse sites, and the board is required to follow their wish.

Payment of Teachers' Pensions. Pensions to teachers are of recent acquisition to the purposes for which school funds may be devoted. Even now they are not common to every state. In states where legislation has been enacted providing for payment of such bounties to teachers either by the state or by the municipality or school district, such legislation provides either by express words or by implication that it is not a wrongful use of school funds to pay such pensions. This principle is based on the grounds that pensions are part of the salary consideration of the teacher for service rendered, and therefore a legitimate expenditure.[50] The difficulties encountered in adjusting pension cases arise out of conditions peculiar to each state or locality. Frequently the point at issue is whether the pension shall be or

[49] Reams *v.* Town of McMinnville, 291 S. W. (Tenn.) 1067; University of Knoxville *v.* Knoxville, 6 Baxt. 166; Newman *v.* Ashe, 9 Baxt. 380; Grove *v.* Peoria Board of School Inspectors, 20 Ill. 532.

[50] Mahan *v.* Board of Education, 171 N. Y. 263; State *v.* Hauge, 37 N. D. 583, 164 N. W. 289.

is retroactive with respect to those teachers who were formerly members of the teaching staff, but are now retired. The general rule in such cases is that pension laws are not retroactive and that, where by special legislation retired teachers are granted a form of payment, it is a mere gratuity and not a pension.

Payment of Counsel Fees. School boards are corporate bodies and can sue and be sued. Such being the case, for the protection of the legal rights of the district, it is generally held that the board has the right to expend funds for counsel fees. Statutes vary a great deal regarding such use of public funds and are construed in the light of the conditions they are made to fit.[51] The fees must be for legitimate counsel service to the district.

Funds Raised by Taxation in One District Expended in Another

Although a certain decision [52] lays down the principle that the people of one district cannot be taxed for the benefit of another district, there are many controlling conditions that demand qualification of the rule. The legislature, restricted only by the constitution, is supreme in its control over taxation. Since it has the power to levy taxes for all public purposes, it has the corresponding power of apportioning the funds so raised if it so wills. In fact any tax laid over a broad area may be said to benefit one portion at the expense of the other. State taxation has for its purpose the aiding of the weak community with funds contributed by the strong. The legislatures may, without the consent of the local school districts, appropriate their funds even though in so doing some of the funds raised in one district are devoted to the use of another district.[53] This does not mean that the power of the legislature is absolutely unrestricted to the point of demanding that one district levy taxes to support another. It does mean that the legislative power extends to the appropriation of the aggregate of taxes raised and that it does not particularly matter whether taxes gathered from one district *in toto* are returned thereto or whether some of them are used for the benefit

[51] Mollohan *v.* Cavender, 75 W. Va. 36, 83 S. E. 78.

[52] Duffy *v.* Burrill, 125 N. E. 135, 234 Mass. 42.

[53] Pearson *v.* State, 56 Ark. 148; State *v.* Hauge, 39 N. D. 583; Miller *v.* Korns, 140 N. E. (Ohio) 773.

of another district when overlapping and commingled interests demand such distribution.[54] It would be beyond legislative prerogative to distribute any district's funds without apportioning them back to such district in the same manner as distributed over the whole area benefited.

What power has the district or county board of education to divert funds of one district to use in another? This is an entirely different question. It is not within the power of a board of education to appropriate funds to the use of another district.[55] This does not mean that no circumstances ever arise whereby funds of one district are used by another.

Submission of the Question of the Tax to the Voters of the District

It is not proposed to enter into an analysis of principles covering the whole scope of submission of the question of taxation to the legal voters of the district. Qualifications of voters, methods of submitting the vote, orders for an election, petitions, notice, and the number required to legalize the tax, are all essential requirements in one jurisdiction or another but do not find their place in this study. It must be stated with respect to them, however, that whatever requirements are set up by law must be strictly complied with.

Particularly in city school districts and frequently in less populous units, a levy of school taxes may be made by the officers of the district without a vote of the people. In most jurisdictions there are constitutional, statutory, or charter provisions requiring a vote of the people as a prerequisite for levying a tax, with the general exception of cities as mentioned above. In many states the board may levy up to a certain limit or rate of taxation, and the vote of the people is required to increase such amount or rate. Where required as a prerequisite to the levy of taxes, a levy is void without the election.[56] But mere irregularities in holding an election will not void it nor the tax where no element of ille-

[54] Town of Keene *v.* Town of Roxbury, 126 A. (N. H.) 7.

[55] Pace *v.* County Board of Education, 105 S. E. (Ga.) 366; Raynolds *v.* Swope, 207 P. 581, 28 N. M. 141.

[56] Murphy *v.* Harbison, 29 Ark. 340; Kansas City, etc., R. Co. *v.* Chapin, 162 Mo. 409.

gality pervades it.[57] A tax levied without a vote is not invalidated by an illegal vote authorizing it, because no vote was required. But taxpayers voting on a levy where the school directors had power to levy without their vote makes the levy illegal, the difference being that in the former case the vote was illegal and had no effect, while in the latter it was a legal vote.[58]

When are tax elections void? Where statutes authorize the election to be held at a certain time of year, one held at a different time is invalid.[59] Where election is required for a tax to raise funds for building purposes, and the law requires that plans for the building be submitted prior thereto, such election without any knowledge of what the building would be is void.[60] An election called by notice to be held at a specified place becomes void when held, without notice of change, in another place.[61] The participation of unqualified persons in an election will not render it void if it is possible to ascertain the true vote without them, and the proposition carried by the requisite number of voters.[62]

What power has the board of education over the vote of the people qualified to vote for a levy of taxes? In all cases where it is made a prerequisite to the tax levy that an election be held, the will of the voters becomes the only authority of the board of education. This is not only law but sound reasoning. Were it otherwise, the election would be no more than a farce.

Summary

1. The taxpayer has legal remedies for erroneous taxation, the principal form of which is an injunction to prevent the collection of the tax.

2. Where property has been illegally taken to satisfy a delinquent tax, the taxpayer may recover not only the property but also the costs of recovery.

3. The taxpayer, even though he has participated in the pro-

[57] Trustees of Common School Dist. No. 88 *v.* Garvey, 80 Ky. 159; Hill *v.* Smithville Indep. School Dist., 239 S. W. (Tex.) 987.

[58] Winters *v.* State, 9 Ind. 172; Cedar Rapids, etc., R. Co. *v.* Carroll County, 41 Iowa 153.

[59] Smith *v.* Canyon County, 226 P. (Idaho) 1070.

[60] Randall *v.* School Dist. No. 44, etc., 205 P. (Wash.) 748; Galloway *v.* Board of Education of Brunswick County, 114 S. E. (N. C.) 165.

[61] Wallace *v.* Excise Board of Bryan County, 216 P. 654, 91 Okla. 101.

[62] *Ibid.*

ceedings to impose a tax, is not prevented from bringing action to question the validity of the tax where such tax appears illegal. But no taxpayer can maintain an action on refusal to pay a tax simply because of irregularity of proceedings to which he was a party.

4. Disposition of school funds must be measured by the same tests as that required for levying the tax. If money cannot be raised for a particular purpose, it cannot be appropriated for that purpose if already in the treasury.

5. Where the law requires that as a prerequisite to the valid levy of a tax it be submitted to the voters of the district, all proceedings connected therewith must be strictly observed.

CHAPTER VIII

CONCLUSION

The very life of the public schools depends for its perpetuity upon the support derived from public taxation. Untrained teachers, inadequate equipment, poorly prepared administrators may each seriously cripple the schools. But neither one nor all of them are so destructive as the drying up of the source of revenue. Curtailment of funds will result in inferior teachers, inadequate equipment, and unprepared administrators. The board of education is invested with a trust not short of stupendous in raising and expending the funds required for the schools of a community. The more thoroughly conversant they are with their rights and liabilities, and the more cognizant they are of powers conferred upon them, the better will their service be to those to whom they are responsible.

To acquire a fundamental knowledge of the powers of boards of education, it is necessary to seek the source of that power. No political subdivision of a state has inherent power to tax. That power resides in the state, exercised by the legislature, and restricted only by the constitution. The school district's power of taxation is a delegated one. It must be exercised in strict conformity to every constitutional and statutory requirement. Only the board of education can exercise this delegated power; it may not be redelegated or transferred to other ministerial or executive officers or bodies. These facts should influence the thinking of a board of education in each contemplated act of taxation.

The state's power to tax is supreme to the extent of imposing a tax upon a district over the objection of unappreciative taxpayers when the educational needs of the children are at stake. The school tax must be uniform and equal over the same class of people and property in so far as attainable. One portion of a district cannot be taxed at a higher rate than another. It is an unquestioned principle of law that taxes cannot be imposed for other than a public purpose. This means that private schools cannot share in the public revenue raised in a district for the public schools no matter how laudable their cause nor how necessary they may be to supplement the facilities of the public schools.

Ignorance of the principles governing property that is taxable and the place of taxation may result in both a loss of school revenue and an injustice to property owners. Real estate is taxable where situated, with the exception that in some states land lying in one body and owned by one person, but in more than one school district, is taxed in the district where the owner resides or where the mansion house is located. The nonresident property owner is as liable to the payment of taxes on his property in a school district as is a resident property owner. The nonresident may be either a citizen or an alien, that fact is immaterial. Tangible personal property does not always follow the domicile of the owner for purposes of taxation as is frequently supposed. It may acquire a situs of its own where more or less permanently situated. Even tangible personalty may acquire a business situs different from the domicile of the owner and be there taxed. This principle needs to be impressed on the minds of boards of education in this day of vast interests with much intangible wealth scattered over a state or the nation. Property transferred from one district to another is taxable in the one where located at the time of the tax date or the assessment date. If transferred after the assessment, it is liable for taxes to the original district although not sharing the benefits of that district. The situs of property becomes fixed as of the tax or assessment date. This may cause personal property to sometimes be taxed twice, as when removed from one district after assessment into another district in a different state before its assessment date. Property temporarily in the school district or in transit cannot be taxed there unless remaining long enough to become fixed, or other conditions change its temporary status. The fact that property has been taxed in one locality for a given year does not always relieve it of taxation in another. Property not on the tax rolls cannot be taxed under any consideration until properly placed upon the rolls, listed, and assessed.

Exemptions from taxation find their right to such privilege in the constitution or the statutes. They are based upon ownership, purposes to which devoted, and both combined, according to the wording of the law. Boards of education should be aware of the restrictions surrounding exempt property and should not permit any property to remain untaxed through a false claim of exemption. Although all statutes granting exemptions are to be strictly construed with respect to private property, a more recent tendency is to favor a liberal construction for religious, charitable, benevolent, and educational institutions.

It is common knowledge that public school property is not taxable. But that does not release from taxation property rented by a board of education for school purposes, nor property owned by the district but leased to an individual or corporation for noneducational purposes. The former is taxable to the owner, the latter to the lessee unless a contract provides otherwise.

In most jurisdictions college and private school property, charitable, benevolent, and religious institutions are exempt as to property used exclusively for such purposes as the institution was established. Property contiguous and reasonably necessary for the uses of the institution is also exempt. But property not devoted to the purposes of the institution becomes taxable, as does remote property not necessary for the purposes of the institution. Parsonages do not always stand exempt because the church is exempt. Cemeteries are uniformly exempt from taxation as to all property used for burial purposes, but not always as to property not used or likely to be used for that purpose. But mausoleums erected in exempt cemeteries by a business corporation as a profit-making venture do not thereby become exempt. Fraternal orders in some states are clearly exempt as to all property owned or devoted to the uses of the order, but generally such organizations have difficulty in meriting the exemption privilege because (1) their social activities are tantamount to their charity, (2) much of their property is leased to others for business purposes, (3) other orders are permitted to use their rooms at a rental charge, (4) the accrued benefits are distributed to members only and not to the public. Hospitals are exempt if not conducted as a business enterprise with the intention of making a profit, although incidental profits will not defeat the exemption when the primary purpose is charitable.

The exemption privilege is neither assignable nor transferable. It may be recalled at the will of the state. Exempt property sold to another and devoted to a different purpose loses its exemption rights. Quick recognition of this principle is necessary to impose taxes on property formerly exempt but transferred to purposes or ownership not entitled to exemption.

A valid tax requires a valid tax levy and assessment. Both are indispensable. But the validity of a tax cannot be denied on the grounds that mere irregularities not working an injustice to the taxpayers have attended the proceedings. A fraudulent levy or assessment makes a void tax. Levy in excess of the statutory limit does not usually invalidate the whole tax, but only that part in excess of the legal limit. Boards of education should act upon their rights in such cases and not be inveigled into believing that the whole tax is invalid.

Back assessment of property omitted from the tax rolls is a legal right and may be employed to procure the taxes on property not furnishing its share of the school burden. An excessive levy of taxes, within the statutory limits, cannot be invalidated unless it appears that the board has acted fraudulently or illegally. The mere raising of more taxes than are needed is not a wrongful action of the board of education. In some jurisdictions it is possible to levy taxes at a different rate for school purposes than for other governmental purposes.

Collection of school taxes is made through an agency separate from the district organization. For that reason it is necessary that laws be framed to safeguard the district in the collection of its tax. Collectors are responsible to the board of education for all taxes collected, and for delinquent taxes in many instances, as well as for the accrued interest on delinquent taxes. Legal action may be maintained to enforce collection and recovery of the collected tax from the collector. However, the recovery by the taxpayer of taxes erroneously paid is a matter of difficulty, as is the recovery of taxes paid to one district rightfully belonging to another district.

Boards of education should realize that the taxpayer has legal remedies for erroneous and unlawful taxation. He may sue the district for taxes illegally collected; he may enjoin the collection of an illegal tax or one that will work a hardship upon him and other taxpayers. In like manner, he has legal weapons to enforce his rights against the board of education for improper disposition of the proceeds of the tax after it is gathered and turned over to the district officers. It must be made clear that if taxes cannot be raised for a purpose, money already in the treasury cannot be devoted to that purpose.

Taxes raised in one district cannot be used in another through the powers of the school boards, but the state legislature has power to distribute a tax raised over a wide area so that one district may share some of the funds raised in another. It is not possible within the law to tax a portion of a district for the benefit of the whole unless some special benefit accrues to that portion.

A general knowledge of the principles deduced in this study should impress boards of education with the sanctity of the trust imposed in them as guardians of the property and resources of the schools, all of which exist for the express purpose of providing equal educational opportunities for the nation's children. All taxable property should pay its share of the burden for school support and should pay it in the situs determined by law. Rights of taxpayers should not be violated either by ignorance or caprice.

ABBREVIATIONS

Ala.—Alabama Reports
A.L.R.—American Law Reports
Am.Dec.—American Decisions
Am.Rep.—American Reports
Ariz.—Arizona Reports
Ark.—Arkansas Reports
Atl. or A.—Atlantic Reporter

Cal.—California Reports
Cal.App.—California Appeal Reports
Colo.—Colorado Reports
Conn.—Connecticut Reports
Cyc.—Cyclopedia of Law and Procedure

Del.—Delaware Reports
D.C.—District of Columbia Reports

Fed.Cas.—Federal Cases (U.S.)
Fed. or F.—Federal Reporter
Fla.—Florida Reports

Ga.—Georgia Reports

Ia. or Iowa—Iowa Reports
Ida.—Idaho Reports
Ill.—Illinois Reports
Ill.App.—Illinois Appeal Reports
Ind.—Indiana Reports
Ind.App.—Indiana Appeal Reports

Kan.—Kansas Reports
Ky.—Kentucky Reports
Ky.L.—Kentucky Law Reports

La.—Louisiana Reports
La.Ann.—Louisiana Annual Reports

L.R.A.—Lawyers' Reports Annotated
L.R.A.n.s.—Lawyers' Reports Annotated New Series

Mass.—Massachusetts Reports
Minn.—Minnesota Reports
Mich.—Michigan Reports
Miss.—Mississippi Reports
Mo.—Missouri Reports
Mo.App.—Missouri Appeal Reports
Me.—Maine Reports
Met.—Metcalf's Reports (Mass.)
Md.—Maryland Reports
Mont.—Montana Reports

N.C.—North Carolina Reports
N.D.—North Dakota Reports
N.E.—Northeastern Reporter
Neb.—Nebraska Reports
N.H.—New Hampshire Reports
N.J.L.—New Jersey Law Reports
N.M.—New Mexico Reports
N.W.—Northwestern Reporter
N.Y.—New York Reports
N.Y.App.—New York Appeal Reports
N.Y.S.—New York Supplement Reports
Nev.—Nevada Reports

Ohio St.—Ohio State Reports
Okla.—Oklahoma Reports
Or. or Ore.—Oregon Reports

Pa.—Pennsylvania Reports
Pa.St.—Pennsylvania State Reports
Pac. or P.—Pacific Reporter
Pick.—Pickering's Reports (Mass.)

R.I.—Rhode Island Reports

S.C.—South Carolina Reports
S.D.—South Dakota Reports
S.E.—Southeastern Reporter
So.—Southern Reporter
Sup.Ct.—Supreme Court Reporter
S.W.—Southwestern Reporter

Tenn.—Tennessee Reports
Tex.—Texas Reports
Tex.App.—Texas Appeal Reports
Tex.Civ.App.—Texas Civil Appeal Reports

U.S.—United States Supreme Court Reports
Utah.—Utah Reports

Va.—Virginia Reports
Vt.—Vermont Reports

Wash.—Washington Reports
Wis.—Wisconsin Reports
W.Va.—West Virginia Reports
Wyo.—Wyoming Reports

BIBLIOGRAPHY

LEGAL

BROWNE, WILLIAM W. *The Law of Assessment and Taxation.* Rochester, N. Y.: Williamson & Higbie, 1887.

BURROUGHS, WILLIAM H. *A Treatise on the Law of Taxation as Imposed by the States and Their Municipalities or Other Subdivisions.* New York: Baker, Voorhis & Co., 1877.

COOLEY, THOMAS MCINTYRE. *The Law of Taxation,* 4th ed. Chicago: Callaghan & Co., 1924.

COTHRAN, GEORGE W. *Assessors and Collectors.* Albany and New York: Banks & Brothers, 1899.

DRAKE, J. N. *Taxes, How Assessed and Collected.* New York: Banks & Brothers, 1896.

SPAHR, MARGARET. "The Supreme Court on the Incidence and Effects of Taxation." *Smith College Studies in History,* Vol. 10, Nos. 2, 3, 4, Jan.-July, 1925.

WELTY, DANIEL W. *A Treatise on the Law of Assessments.* New York and Albany: Banks & Brothers, 1886.

WILKINSHAW, R. B. *Taxation of Governmental Agencies.* Columbia University Convers Prize, 1911. Typewritten manuscript.

ECONOMIC

ELY, RICHARD T. *Taxation in American States and Cities.* New York: Thomas Y. Crowell & Co., 1888.

LEAGUE OF NATIONS. Committee of Technical Experts on Double Taxation and Tax Evasion. Publication of The League of Nations. II. Economic and Financial, 1927.

LUTZ, HARLEY L. Public Finance, Part IV. *Taxation.* New York: D. Appleton & Co., 1925.

NATIONAL INDUSTRIAL CONFERENCE BOARD. "Tax Burdens and Exemptions." *Research Report No. 64.* New York: 1923.

NATIONAL TAX ASSOCIATION. *National Tax Association, Proceedings of,* 1907-1924, incl.

NATIONAL TAX ASSOCIATION. "Report of the Committee on Double Taxation and Situs for the Purposes of Taxation." *National Tax Association, Proceedings of, Ninth Conference,* 1915, p. 358.

SELIGMAN, E. R. A. *Essays in Taxation,* 9th ed. New York: Macmillan Company, 1923.

SELIGMAN, E. R. A. *The Shifting and Incidence of Taxation.* New York: Columbia University Press, 1927.

Contains a very complete bibliography on taxation from the economic point of view.

WALKER, F. "Double Taxation in the United States." *Columbia Studies,* Vol. V, No. 1 (1895).

WELLS, DAVID A. *Theory and Practice of Taxation.* New York: D. Appleton & Co., 1900.